EQUITY AND GENDER

This book is sponsored by the Cato Institute

Founded in 1977, the Cato Institute is a public policy research organization dedicated to exploring policy options consistent with the traditional American principles of individual liberty, limited government, and peace.

EQUITY AND GENDER

The Comparable Worth Debate

Ellen Frankel Paul

Transaction Publishers
New Brunswick (U.S.A.) and Oxford (U.K.)

Library of Congress Catalog Number: 88-4760
ISBN 0-88738-204-5 (cloth)
088738-720-9 (paper)
Printed in the United States of America

Library of Congress Cataloging-in-Publication Data

Paul, Ellen Frankel.
    Equity and gender.

    Bibliography: p.
    Includes index.
    1. Pay equity—Law and legislation—United States.
    2. Pay equity—United States. I. Title.
KF3467.P38   344.73′0121   88-4760
ISBN 0-88738-204-5   347.304121
ISBN 0-88738-720-9 (pbk.)

To Kristen Eden Paul

Contents

Acknowledgements

James Dorn and David Boaz of the Cato Institute displayed great patience and encouragement throughout the writing—or for long stretches of time— non-writing of this book. For their patience, no less than their editorial skill, I wish to thank them most sincerely.

Carol Olson, staff research analyst for the Iowa Senate Republican caucus and Malcolm J. Sherman, Assistant to the Staff Director of the United States Commission on Civil Rights were very helpful in providing me with key pieces of information at precisely the moments I needed them to avoid panic.

Several people at the Social Philosophy and Policy Center were helpful either in a research or secretarial capacity, and their assistance, too, is greatly appreciated. They are: Kory Tilgner, Pat Steinbauer, Tamara Sharp, and Terrie Weaver.

Introduction

Comparable worth, or pay equity in its newer guise, is an attractive concept: if only employers could be required to pay female employees in traditionally female occupations the same salaries as males in male-dominated jobs of comparable value to their employers, then the "wage gap" would largely disappear. Advocates for women's equality have become increasingly enthusiastic about this strategy for achieving their goals, as they have seen other legal remedies—the Equal Pay Act, Title VII of the Civil Rights Act—fail to secure to women this elusive equality.

Comparable worth in the 1980s has achieved remarkable strides, virtually sweeping the country. Despite comparable worth's seeming novelty—it is a concept that has caught fire only recently—the idea has been around for quite a while. In fact, the notion of "comparable work" was employed by the National War Labor Board during World War II. The board required equal pay for "comparable work" and made job evaluations within plants between dissimilar jobs to determine whether any pay inequities existed. Every Congress since 1945 has entertained a comparable work bill of various types.[1]

"Equal pay for equal work" is not the objective of the comparable worth advocates, for that standard has been the law of the land since 1963, when the Equal Pay Act was approved by Congress as an amendment to the Fair Labor Standards Act. Since then, it has been illegal to pay women less than men doing "substantially equal" work.[2] For many advocates of women's equality, however, this standard does not go nearly far enough. It leaves important gaps in the protection afforded to women workers; for example, women who labor in jobs with no equivalent male jobs available for purposes of comparison are left unprotected as are women whose work is comparable to men's but not equal by the "substantially equal" standard. If over half the women in the United States work in jobs that are 75% dominated by women, then more must be done to alleviate their lot than simply securing them equal pay for equal work.[3]

However, comparable worth's advocates are not merely pointing to a lacunae in the law. They seek sweeping reforms that would question the very

1

foundation of our market-based economic system. What they doubt is not the efficiency of the market but its justice. Why, they ask, should a female registered nurse whose skills require years of training and whose responsibility for the preservation of human life is so great be paid less than a garbage man? Why should a social worker, another female-dominated job classification, receive less pay than a truck driver, when the social worker requires years of schooling and must exercise considerable judgment in guiding the lives of others? Why do women working full-time earn a mere 64 cents to men's one dollar? Something must be radically amiss in a market system that produces such patent inequities, the advocates conclude.

The market, as the comparable worth supporters view it, is corrupted by discrimination, for nothing else can sufficiently explain the discrepancies between women's wages and men's. As Joy Ann Grune, former executive director of the National Committee on Pay Equity, one of the leading activist groups, wrote:

> Culture, history, psychiatry, and social relations all have a role in wage discrimination, as they do in other legal rights issues. They contribute to the creation and maintenance of a gender-based division of labor in the market economy that is old, pronounced, and pays women less.[4]

The market, Grune contends, will not spontaneously eliminate this alleged discrimination. Even when an employer acts to set wages with a nondiscriminatory intent, if that employer uses prevailing market standards as his guide, those wages will reflect the prior discriminatory evaluations of other employers. Thus, remediation is necessary by governmental actions to break this chain of perpetuated inequities.

Court cases have lent considerable encouragement to the supporters of comparable worth. *County of Washington v. Gunther*, decided by the Supreme Court in 1981, breathed new life into the comparable worth movement, opening the door for suits under Title VII of the Civil Rights Act of 1964 that would allow claims of something more than "equal pay for equal work," the standard set by the Equal Pay Act.[5]

While *Gunther* gave hope to comparable worth proponents, it was not an endorsement of the concept nor was it a clear signal that comparable worth claims would fall under Title VII. The decision sets no criteria for which claims in addition to "equal pay for equal work" might fall under Title VII. It certainly does not set definitive standards, as the dissenters pointed out. Indeed, the majority at several points in the decision disclaimed any relation of their decision to the comparable worth theory.[6]

In 1983, taking cognizance of the window of opportunity provided by *Gunther*, Judge Tanner of the United States District Court of the Western District of Washington decided a case, *American Federation of State, County, and*

Municipal Employees (AFSCME) v. Washington,[7] which invigorated the movement even more. In that case, the judge held that the State of Washington, which had instituted a series of comparable worth studies beginning in 1974, had to implement these findings. The plaintiffs, the class of those in female-dominated job classifications, were awarded back pay, injunctive relief, and a declaratory judgment that the state was in violation of Title VII.

AFSCME v. Washington seemed to fulfill the promise held out to comparable worth advocates by *Gunther*. By the time the Ninth Circuit Court of Appeals heard and finally overturned the ruling on September 4, 1985,[8] the comparable worth forces had become so strong, both in the state and national political arenas, that the decision served not to seriously wound the movement, but rather to further inspire the troops. Eleanor Smeal, President of the National Organization of Women (NOW), responded to the ruling in fighting spirit, declaring that NOW must work "on several fronts simultaneously and . . . the movement must raise hell." She blamed the setback on intensive lobbying by business:

> Courts don't operate in a vacuum. The business community has been making its case for months on end that it's OK to discriminate if everyone does. The court bought that line. Well, we don't accept that. We're going to the Supreme Court. If that court buys the line, then we're going to the Congress and raise so much hell they'll be compelled to change it. We simply won't accept a ruling that justifies injustice.[9]

Comparable worth's greatest victories to date have come at the state level, with ten states (Hawaii, Iowa, Maine, Michigan, Minnesota, Montana, Ohio, Oregon, Washington, and Wisconsin) already implementing the results of comparable worth studies. At least twenty-seven states have conducted evaluations of their pay scales to determine whether they are influenced by sex-based discrimination, with twenty states having conducted studies explicitly based on the comparable worth concept.[10]

At the local level, too, pay equity is finding converts. In May 1985, the City of Los Angeles instituted a plan to raise the salaries of 3,900 workers in female-dominated job categories; the three-year plan is designed to raise wages by 10% to 15%. And in the November 1986 election, the voters of San Francisco approved a city charter amendment that calls for the implementation of pay equity wage increases upon the conclusion of a survey comparing the wages of female- and minority-dominated job classes to white-male-dominated classes.

At the federal level, too, comparable worth has achieved some modest successes, with bills calling for comparable worth studies of the federal bureaucracy having passed the House both in 1984 and 1985 by overwhelming majorities. On June 28, 1984, for example, H.R. 5680, the "Federal Pay Equity and Management Improvement Act'' passed the House by a vote of 413 to 6, and it was the first bill calling for an element of comparable worth to ever pass in either chamber. It did not survive the reconciliation process, under heavy pressure from the Reagan administration, particularly the Office of Personnel Management.

Again in 1985, the House passed a comparable worth bill that also called for a study, but was now broadened to include not only sex-based discrimination in wages, but racial and national origin-based discrimination as well. The legislation, H.R. 3008, was sponsored by Rep. Mary Rose Oakar (D.- Ohio) a tireless worker on behalf of pay equity. The bill called for the formation of an 11-member commission to evaluate federal wage and classification systems. The vote this time was less lopsided, but still a convincing 259-162, with 23 Democrats and 139 Republicans voting against the bill. The identical measure introduced in the Senate by Senators Alan Cranston (D-Calif.) and Daniel Evans (R-Wash.) died in the Senate Governmental Affairs Committee.

The opponents of these bills—business groups, the Reagan administration, and many congressional Republicans—argued that the call for a study was not as innocuous as it might seem on first impression, since it would set the groundwork for lawsuits demanding that the government pay billions in back pay and pay raises (much like the scenario in the State of Washington).

Numerous other bills have been introduced in both houses of Congress during the last few years, with mainly Republican opposition in the Senate dooming all of them. The latest effort was an attempt in the Senate in the fall of 1986 to attach a bill, S.519, to a continuing resolution; this bill failed to make it out of committee and did not succeed as a floor amendment. This bill called not only for a comparable worth study, but also for the director of the Office of Personnel Management to prepare a plan and timetable for the implementation of the recommendations of the consultant selected by a nine-member Commission on Compensation Equity.

Comparable worth, while it began in the public sector and has enjoyed its greatest successes there, is not a concept to be limited to government employment. Rather, its proponents wish to extend its purview eventually to all labor markets. In one state, Pennsylvania, legislation was pending in 1985 to do precisely that. Hawaii has passed a nonbinding resolution encouraging all employers to adopt a comparable worth standard. The public sector is simply the starting point for a much more ambitious effort to eradicate alleged discriminatory wage patterns. Since the public sector employs wage grades for classifying and paying its employees, this arena is the natural choice for launching the comparable worth campaign.

If the market is defective due to historical and present discrimination, then some mechanism must be found to supplant, or at the very least replace, this wage-setting system with one that is more equitable. Pay equity advocates find this new mechanism in evaluation schemes that are, they say, more objective than the market. For example, the State of Washington engaged the consulting firm of Norman Willis & Associates when it performed its first comparable worth study in 1974. The Willis study used a methodology similar to that used in comparable worth studies by other consulting firms (such as Hay Associates, which has done extensive work in this area). Each employment classification was assessed on the basis of four factors: (1) *Knowledge and Skills* (job knowledge, interpersonal communication skills, coordinating skills); (2) *Mental Demands* (independent judgment, decision making, problem solving requirements); (3) *Accountability* (freedom to take action, nature of the job's impact, size of the job's impact); and (4) *Working Conditions* (physical efforts, hazards, discomfort, environmental conditions).[11]

Evaluation committees assessed job classifications on these four criteria and awarded points to each. Comparable jobs, then, were those that achieved approximately the same overall point scores. In this way, such disparate jobs as secretary, nurse, surveyor, highwayman, etc. could be compared. This methodology attempts to replace subjective and, hence, discriminatory market decisions with objective, measurable, nondiscriminatory assessments by trained evaluators.

This claim that objectivity is attainable in evaluating the worth of all individuals' work is what the proponents of pay equity find so attractive. The vagaries, idiosyncrasies, and outright discrimination that are embedded in the marketplace can be replaced by the objective determinations of experts. Discrimination, by this device of comparable worth evaluations, can finally be overcome, and women placed on an equal footing in the labor market with men; the wage gap, or at least that portion of it that is attributable to discrimination, will finally be eliminated.

For its supporters, women's rights groups, political parties and politicians, and many unions[12]—such groups as NOW, AFSCME, the National Committee on Pay Equity, the NAACP Legal Defense Fund, the U.S. Conference of Mayors, the Mondale-Ferraro Democratic presidential ticket of 1984, the Democratic National Platform of 1984, the National Commission on Working Women, and numerous others[13]—comparable worth provides the hope of a quick and relatively easy fix for the injustice foisted upon women by the marketplace. And, indeed, comparable worth when fought for on the barricades, so to speak, has produced some notable successes. In San Jose, Calif., the municipal workers struck for nine days in 1981 and achieved a promise from the city to provide $1.5 million in pay adjustments to women workers to reduce the effects of alleged discrimination. Had the District Court decision in *AFSCME v. Washington* been upheld, the state would have had to pay an estimated $800 million in back pay and raises.

Given the sweeping changes that comparable worth might bring about (and the extent of those changes is in dispute), it is not surprising that the movement has engendered a considerable amount of opposition from business groups (such as the U.S. Chamber of Commerce), politicians (the Reagan administration), and academics.

An enormous body of literature has been generated in the last five years on comparable worth. Most of it from the academic community is sympathetic to the notion, but some of it stands in opposition. A detailed analysis of the opposition's arguments against pay equity will be reserved for later treatment; for now it will suffice to briefly discuss the general outlines of the opponents' views. Both the activists and the academic critics attack comparable worth from a similar perspective, namely an economic one: that comparable worth would disrupt the marketplace and replace the free choice of individuals about wage bargains with the edicts of government experts.

The critics try to explain the "wage gap" away by isolating differences between the way men and women labor and the kinds of jobs they freely choose. Since the "wage gap" forms such an important datum upon which the proponents base their case for comparable worth, I will examine later in detail the merits of each sides' contentions.

Comparable worth studies based on job evaluations form another critical element in the advocates' position. But the opponents challenge the objectivity of such studies, claiming that they are based on the merely arbitrary and subjective judgments of so-called experts. They contrast studies like the one done in Washington State with job evaluations performed by individual firms, studies that take into account the forces of supply and demand and the objectives of the company.

More fundamentally, the critics challenge the notion that jobs have an "inherent worth." Rather, they contend, jobs are worth what they will command in the market as the result of a freely negotiated wage bargain and nothing more can be said about worth. Frequently, they deride the pay equity enthusiasts as unknowingly harkening back to a Medieval notion of "just price": that price must be something inherent and that it ought to be fixed by a guild with the power to punish transgressors who dare to sell at any other price.

The critics are also concerned that if comparable worth were mandated in the private sector, it would raise the cost of production and, thus, raise domestic prices while further impairing our ability to compete on international markets. Some critics worry, too, that women will be discouraged from entering male-dominated occupations if a comparable worth strategy is pursued, rolling back the progress that has been made in the last decade as women have in increasing numbers penetrated formerly male bastions. And others fear that, despite the protestations of pay equity advocates that they do not wish to lower the wages of males, such will be inevitable as comparable worth dictates that women's salaries must be raised.

Critics have estimated that the price tag for imposing comparable worth on the U.S. economy would be somewhere around $300 billion. This would cause tremendous disruption in the economy. Furthermore, they argue, it would particularly harm women's employment prospects; if secretaries must be paid more than their market value, then some secretaries will be fired, to be replaced by word processors.

On the legal front, comparable worth would penalize employers for wage-setting practices over which they have little control, thus violating one of the principles of our legal system—that individuals should be penalized only for actions in which they are at fault. Pay equity for women would hurt blue-collar men, and blue-collar women also, because Willis-type schemes seem to favor education and other easily measured skills over manual labor.

In the chapters that follow, I will evaluate the economic and pragmatic arguments of both sides of the comparable worth debate. I will also describe the legal background to the debate, legislative developments on the state and national levels, and judicial decisions. But the merits of the comparable worth concept do not, I will argue, lie primarily in economic arguments or disputes about the practical consequences of implementing such a reform. The comparable worth activists are right in one respect at least: justice and equity must triumph over considerations of efficiency. Thus, Winn Newman, AFSCME's lawyer in its case against the State of Washington, had his priorities right when he said: "Ending discrimination costs money, but no one would dare raise that as a reason for continuing to pay blacks less than whites."[14]

In other words, if right lies on the side of comparable worth, then comparable worth should prevail. The only remaining question, then, would be "how can it be implemented in the least disruptive manner?"

Notes

1. *County of Washington v. Gunther*, 452 U.S. 161 (1981), Rehnquist dissent at 185 n. 1.
2. The Equal Pay Act is Section 6 of the Fair Labor Standards Act of 1938. The "substantially equal" definition of equal work is judicially defined language. See: *Shultz v. Wheaton Glass Co.*, 421 F. 2d 259, *cert. denied*, 398 U.S. 905 (1970); *Brennan v. Prince William Hospital Corp.*, 503 F. 2d 282, *cert. denied*, 420 U.S. 972 (1975).
3. *Who's Working for Working Women*, National Committee on Pay Equity and the National Women's Political Caucus, 1984.
4. Joy Ann Grune, "Pay Equity is a Necessary Remedy for Wage Discrimination," in *Comparable Worth: Issues for the 80s*, A Consultation of the U.S. Commission on Civil Rights, June 6-7, 1984, p. 165.
5. *County of Washington v. Gunther*, 452 U.S. 161 (1981).
6. E.g. at 757: "We emphasize at the outset the narrowness of the question before us in this case. Respondents' claim is not based on the controversial concept of 'comparable worth' . . ."

7. *American Federation of State, County, and Municipal Employees v. State of Washington*, 578 F. Supp. 846 (1983).
8. *American Federation of State, County, and Municipal Employees v. Washington*, 770 F. 2d 1401 (1985).
9. "NOW to Fight Comparable Worth Ruling," UPI, September 6, 1985.
10. "Pay Equity: Status of State Activity," GAO report as discussed in "Comparable Worth: Still the Subject of Studies, Bargaining," *Fair Employment Practices* 123 (October 16, 1986). It is difficult to say with certainty how many states have adopted pay equity requirements: other sources list Idaho, New Mexico, and South Dakota among the states that have implemented comparable worth. See: "In Minnesota, 'Pay Equity' Passes Test, but Foes See Trouble Ahead," *The Wall Street Journal*, May 10, 1985. What can be said with assurance is that the movement at the state level is gaining momentum.
11. *AFSCME v. State of Washington*, at 865 n. 9.
12. Union support deserves further explanation. Unions in the United States have, historically, not been terribly hospitable to the entry of women into male-dominated occupations. The numerous cases brought against unions under Title VII of the Civil Rights Act of 1964 is vivid evidence of this history. Recent developments, however, have made many unions cognizant of the need to serve women workers to ensure their own survival: jobs in heavy industry are evaporating while white-collar jobs held mainly by women are proliferating. Unions must now serve a changing constituency, and comparable worth is one way of pleasing many unions' female constituency. Thus, in the current environment that unions such as AFSCME face, it is not remarkable at all that many of them are at the forefront of the forces supporting comparable worth. The unions that are most active in behalf of comparable worth are those with large female memberships whose wages would be raised if comparable worth were implemented. Unions traditionally have attempted to raise their members' wages, even at the cost of fewer jobs (e.g., the United Auto Workers in recent years). For male-dominated unions, comparable worth would serve to limit the number of women entering traditionally male jobs.
13. Other groups that support comparable worth include: the National Institute for Women of Color, the Comparable Worth Project (Oakland, California), Women Employed, Women's Equity Action League, and the Women's Legal Defense Fund.
14. As quoted in "Equal Pay for 'Comparable Worth' Growing as Job-Discrimination Issue," *New York Times*, September 4, 1984, p. 17.

1

The Case for Comparable Worth

Comparable worth deserves a fair hearing—a dispassionate examination, free from the acrimony of much that has passed for public debate on this subject. For those who have endorsed comparable worth, enthusiasm for the concept is born of a perception that women have not enjoyed the full fruits of the U.S. economic system. To rectify this imbalance in economic rewards between men and women workers, something beyond benign neglect and the workings of the marketplace must be relied upon. Simply permitting the market to operate unencumbered by governmental intervention on behalf of women's paychecks will not suffice. That women who advocate comparable worth sincerely believe they are the victims of injustice cannot be denied, and it is for this reason that comparable worth deserves serious consideration: have women been unfairly treated in the U.S. marketplace; if they have, is comparable worth the appropriate remedy?

Comparable worth's supporters respond to the first question with an unqualified ''yes,'' while in answer to the second, they see comparable worth as an equitable and feasible remedy. We will examine the case for comparable worth—not the case of any particular advocate for the cause, but rather a compilation of the typical kinds of arguments that comparable worth's advocates advance—as it proceeds from an indictment of the U.S. marketplace's treatment of women workers to an endorsement of a radical new remedy, pay equity. We will examine in some detail the workings of actual pay equity evaluation schemes in the states, as well as the theory that underlies their construction.

Throughout, comparable worth, with its attempt to provide objective standards to measure job skills and place all types of labor in an enterprise on a similar, measurable scale, will be presented in its most attractive guise. The arguments of comparable worth's critics shall be reserved for Chapter 2.

Discrimination and the Marketplace: Are Women Treated Unfairly?

Contrary to the view held by enthusiasts of the marketplace—that markets, if left free of governmental intervention, tend to minimize discrimination over

9

the long run—supporters of comparable worth view the marketplace as permeated by discrimination.

Discrimination can manifest itself in several forms. The crudest and most overt sort of discrimination is that represented by entry-level barriers against women or minorities and hindrances to promotion once hired. Title VII of the Civil Rights Act of 1964 addressed these sorts of discrimination and made their practice illegal, thus giving protected groups legal redress against patently discriminatory employment practices.

Another more subtle form of discrimination exists, comparable worth advocates say, when individuals are paid less for performing jobs simply because they exhibit certain social characteristics deemed undesirable by mainstream U.S. society. Since the mainstream of the work force is still dominated by white males, the social attributes considered less desirable are being black, being female, and especially being black and female.

One form of wage discrimination, again the most overt, has been illegal since 1963 and the passage of the Equal Pay Act. But that act only barred a narrow band of discriminatory wage setting, that which fell afoul of the "equal pay for equal work standard." This, however, leaves unprotected those members of disfavored groups who are not performing essentially the same jobs as a white male.

For the large majority of women who perform traditionally female jobs—nurses, secretaries, elementary school teachers, social workers, day care attendants—their problem in achieving fair treatment in the marketplace for wages is not addressed by the Equal Pay Act's prohibition. Their lowly wage scales can only be remedied by a comparable-worth type standard.

Whether employers intend to discriminate is irrelevant to this type of analysis; simply by paying prevailing market rates for female-dominated job categories, employers incorporate the discriminatory animus of the general population against the kind of work women have traditionally performed.

Under comparable-worth analysis, wage discrimination arises "when the job structure within a firm is substantially segregated by sex, race, or ethnicity, and workers of one category are paid less than workers of another category when the two groups are performing work that is not the same but that is, in some sense, of comparable worth to their employer."[1] Paula England, a professor of sociology and political economy at the University of Texas at Dallas, most succinctly captures the type of discrimination comparable worth aims to eradicate when she writes: "This type of sex discrimination occurs when the sex composition of jobs influences what employers are willing to pay those who do the jobs, whether this influence is conscious or unconscious."[2]

The marketplace systematically undervalues the work of women and minorities simply because that work is performed by members of disfavored groups. If white males predominated in the vocations of nurse or secretary, these job categories would be paid more.[3] This is the kind of discrimination the market has failed to address.

Why has this market failure persisted? While free-market enthusiasts argue that discriminatory hiring and wage-setting behavior tends to disappear over time because it impairs the competitiveness of those who do the discriminating, comparable worth's economic analysis of the market is quite different. Where market economists see fluidity in labor markets and workers availing themselves of numerous options for employment, the comparable-worth analysis of the market sees rigidities and workers constrained by limited options.

Comparable worth's partisans, borrowing much of their analysis from the resurgent school of institutional economics,[4] see the market as burdened by barriers to the entry of labor, including labor unions, which for much of their history have been hostile to women and often completely barred their entry to certain occupations or abetted employers in sequestering women in the lowest paying jobs.

Employers, too, take their share of the blame for undervaluing women's abilities, their commitment to remaining in the labor force, and their desire for upward advancement. Both groups—unions as well as employers—are dominated by the same privileged social group: white males. For both, then, the desire is strong to monopolize the skills and educational advantages necessary to enter and advance in the most desirable and remunerative occupations. The "old boy network" operated, and still operates, to sequester women in the less desirable vocations and to limit the advancement of even those select females who happen to penetrate heretofore all male bastions.

Nancy Reder, of the National Committee for Pay Equity, agrees that the market does not work as freely as comparable worth's critics contend. "I don't buy the argument that we have a classic free marketplace," she argues. As evidence of this claim, she cites the example of the shortage of engineers, a predominantly male profession, compared with the shortage of nurses. The market's response is different: "The wages offered to engineers go up, while nurses who will work cheap are imported from abroad. We have to recognize that is the pattern, not a fluke."[5]

Beyond the economic barrier to entry and advancement that women suffer is an additional impediment that is more intangible, even psychological. Women have been skewed by a hostile, discriminatory environment to expect that their options will be limited to traditionally feminine roles, born of women's historical function as the nurturing element in the family.[6] As an outgrowth of women's role in the home as care giver for the children and as helpmate for the husband as he pursues his career in the business world, women are conditioned to expect that when they do enter the world of work it will be in a supportive capacity. Thus, women have their options limited and their expectations truncated at an early age. They are told to become helpmates in the work place—and they see women performing these ancillary duties and doing little else—to become the secretaries, nurses, and child-care providers. When women, falling victim to such limited expectations, enter their educational careers, they naturally cleave to the "softer" disciplines and eschew courses in engineering, the sciences. and business, courses that would prepare them to compete in professions dominated by men.

Helen Remick, director of the Office for Affirmative Action at the University of Washington, persuasively articulates this complaint of women being channeled by society into becoming the helpmates of men:

> Have nurses, dental hygienists, clerical workers, and other daughters been similarly trained as helpmates rather than doers? Have we been subtly and not so subtly denied the secrets, the essence of knowledge, being given only as much as others thought we need to know? Is this another form of protection without which we would be better off . . . ? Virtually all women's work suffers from the cultural perceptions that its main purpose is to help, not to do, and that there need to be men around to tell women what to do. These beliefs lead naturally to an assumption that women's work deserves little compensation; any woman could do it (with a little help from a man), and it is inherently rewarding.[7]

Thus, the literacy requirements of secretaries are underestimated, as well as the teaching skills of day care workers and the responsibilities of mothering.[8]

From their earliest years, even before secondary school or college, women experience these subtle forms of discrimination that shape them to be less competitive then their male peers. In the Little Leagues and competitive sports arenas that have historically been closed to women, boys learn to compete and to hone their aggressive skills. Women, in contrast, are taught to be passive and to develop their supportive skills in home economics courses and more covertly in the feedback they get from teachers. Thus instilled with passivity, women confront employers with lower expectations than their male competitors. Women are willing to accept lower compensation than men because they have been taught to value themselves less highly.

Sharon Toffey Shepela, director of the Women's Research Institute of Hartford College and a professor of psychology, and her coauthor, Ann Viviano, are two comparable worth supporters who place considerable weight on these psychological arguments. They employ such tools to help explain both the occupational segregation and the wage differentials that women experience to their detriment. They advance the hypothesis that:

> Women are paid less because they are in women's jobs, and women's jobs are paid less because they are done by women. The reason is that women's work—in fact, virtually anything done by women—is characterized as less valuable. In addition, the characteristics attributed to women are those our society values less.[9]

In support of this hypothesis, they examine studies that show that people react differently to infants depending on the sex the interviewer attributes to the baby and other studies that demonstrate that subjects attribute different worth to job applicants with identical backgrounds depending on the sex that is randomly assigned to them. They cite other studies, which indicate that textbooks exhibit extreme stereotyping of women, picturing them in a limited number of roles as compared to men, and engaging most frequently in passive, docile, and dependent behavior; that teachers treat boys and girls differently; that work by males is evaluated more favorably than women's, with the underlying assumption that the male is more competent; that a male's performance is more likely to be attributed to ability, while a female's accomplishment is attributed to luck. They concluded their psychological analysis of the impediments suffered by women in the work force with this sobering statement:

> We have shown that there are deeply ingrained, pervasive psychological biases that affect decisions made about the competence and work of women. Women's work is everywhere devalued. The subtle forces that we hypothesize to be in part responsible for continued gender-based wage discrimination will be difficult to eradicate, but their effects have been well documented. Those trying to develop equitable compensation systems must assume that bias will be in operation and control its effects as best they can.[10]

As a response to this systemic discrimination—this patterning of women by society to expect less of themselves, combined with the more overt forms of discrimination they suffer when the male establishment values their work less than the work performed by men—the comparable worth advocates seek to persuade or compel employers to adopt a unified value system. Only in this way will wage discrimination be eliminated.

Ronnie Steinberg, director of the Program on Comparable Worth for the Center for Women in Government at the State University of New York at Albany, argues that the kind of wage discrimination women suffer really amounts to an inconsistent application of the values an employer rewards in his work force or an inappropriate assessment of the worth of various jobs done primarily by men and women. Rather than representing an alternative reward system to the market, she contends that comparable worth would merely ensure that employers rewarded all of their workers on the same value scale:

> The values or standards in question are those of the employer as reflected in a firm's wage structure. Thus, comparable worth policy does not fly in the face of the market principle of basing wages on the productive contribution of a job to a firm. Rather, like other equal employment policies, it seeks to differentiate market-based values and standards from discrimination.[11]

Other supporters of women's rights, however, dissent from Steinberg's moderate view that comparable worth will not really impose a different standard but only make employers hew to values they already embrace in compensating male employees. Daphne Greenwood, an economist, is one of them. She argues that the comparable worth concept represents a fundamental reappraisal of what value is and an indictment of how the market sets value; thus, it is more than an equal opportunity policy.[12]

For supporters of comparable worth, then, the market is riddled with discrimination, some of it addressed by the anti-discrimination legislation of the early 1960s, but much of it left undisturbed, to linger on as vestiges of an oppressive, male-dominated society. Now, let us examine in more detail the evidence adduced by the comparable worth advocates to buttress this vision of U.S. society as permeated by an animus against women in the work place.

The Wage Gap

One of the most striking and seemingly compelling charges of the comparable worth advocates is that women who work full-time receive a mere 60 cents for every dollar earned by men.[13] This 60 cent figure has become a rallying cry for women's rights groups, who point out that, despite the enactment of equal opportunity laws in the early 1960s, women have still remained in this disadvantaged position. Indeed, if all workers are taken into account—full-time as well as part-time—the disparity widens even more: to 50 cents for women to men's one dollar. What accounts for this is the greater tendency of women to engage in part-time work.

This disparity between men's and women's wages has tended to persist over time, hovering at around the 60 cents mark. For example, in 1970 the figure stood at 59 cents, while in 1981 it had risen to only 62 cents.[14] Back through the 1960s, too, the disparity floated around the 60 cent figure. Despite the Equal Pay Act of 1963 and Title VII the following year, women's wages have not noticeably risen as a proportion of the earnings of men.

What adds urgency to the 60 cents sloganeering is the increased labor force participation of women over the last few decades. In 1960, only 23 million women worked, a mere 37.7% of their numbers, while by 1983, 53% of women worked, and by 1981 they comprised 43% of all workers.

What makes these figures even more compelling is the dramatic increase in the number of women with children who now labor in the marketplace. As just one indicant of this growth, the percentage of women with children under three who work has increased from 34% in 1975 to 50.8% in 1986.[15] This huge increase in the number of women with very young children who have entered the marketplace indicates to many that work for women has become a necessity rather than a frivolity, a need to express themselves, or a mere supplement to the family income. Rather, women work today in large part because their incomes have become a necessity for their families. Whether from divorce or the ravages of the high inflation of the 1970s, women's work has become vital to the welfare of the American family. If women constitute such an important component of the labor force in the 1980s, why should they not be remunerated on the same basis as their male colleagues? Such is the query of the women's groups and their supporters who clamor for change in the U.S. marketplace.

Publicists for comparable worth who air their appeals in the media tend to use the 60 cent figure in its unvarnished form. They do not consider any factors that may serve to explain part of the wage gap, for to do so would, of course, blunt the force of their argument. If the wage gap were a mere 10% or 15%, rather than the striking figure of 40%, and if, furthermore, the extent of the 10% that is due to discrimination rather than some other factors were debatable, the case for comparable worth would become much too murky to serve the cause.

Typical of the treatment of the wage gap in public debate is a pamphlet produced by the National Committee on Pay Equity, titled "The Wage Gap: Myths and Facts." It begins with the refrain that while women are performing many of the most important jobs in the nation—as teachers, nurses, and secretaries—they are paid 61 cents for every dollar paid to men. This figure is somewhat higher in the governmental sector, but in the private sector it is even worse: only 56 cents.

The pamphlet then proceeds to explode some common myths about the wage gap:

(1) *The average earnings of women are increasing relative to men.* No, the gap has actually widened slightly since the 1930s, with the figure standing at 63.6 in 1939 and 59.2 in 1981.

(2) *Women are paid less because of differences in education and work experience.* This, too, is found to be fallacious, as differences in these factors are insufficient to explain the wage gap, accounting for perhaps a quarter but certainly not more than half of the gap. Women with college degrees earned less than men with high school diplomas; women at every educational level received less pay then men of equal schooling. In 1981, both men and women employed in the work place had completed the same median level of education: 12.7 years.

(3) *Women and men have come close to achieving equality in the kinds of jobs they hold.* On the contrary, women have been segregated in a small number of occupations. According to Department of Labor statistics, of the twelve major job occupations, 52% of all working women labor in two of the twelve categories—clerical workers and service workers. Of the 427 subcategories of job classifications, 50% of employed women work in only twenty occupations. "In 1982, more than half of all em-

ployed women worked in occupations which are 75% female, and 22% of employed women were in jobs that are more than 95% female. . . . It is especially important to note that the entry of women into predominantly male professional and blue collar jobs has *not* reduced the overall degree of segregation.''[16]

(4) *People are paid what their jobs are worth*. False again. To make the case, the National Committee cites three job evaluation studies done on a comparable worth theory: those conducted by Hay Associates for Minnesota and the city of San Jose, Calif., and the Willis study commissioned by the State of Washington. These studies awarded points to job factors and then compared the actual salaries of jobs that came out in the study to have the same number of points. Female-dominated jobs invariably received less pay than male jobs.[17]

Scholars in the academy who support comparable worth, pressed by the efforts of the concept's opponents to shrink the apparent wage gap, have entered the fray on a more sophisticated level than the activist groups. Through use of regression analysis and other statistical techniques, they have also shrunk the wage gap, but their efforts have not dissuaded them from support for comparable worth. Instead, they typically attribute to discrimination whatever wage gap they cannot explain away as due to other factors.

Let us examine some typical efforts at decomposing the wage gap. Treiman and Hartmann, in their study commissioned by the Equal Employment Opportunity Commission (EEOC) and the Department of Labor, conclude that only a small part of the earning differential between men and women can be accounted for by "differences in education, labor force experience, labor force commitment, or other human capital factors believed to contribute to productivity differences among workers." Studies that employ such methodology "usually account for less than a quarter and never more than half of the observed earnings differences."[18]

They go on to suggest that another component of the wage gap may be attributed to the fact that women are concentrated in low-paying jobs. They see few signs of this job segregation diminishing. By employing an institutional approach, they argue that it is likely that the differential can be attributed in part to discrimination, both intentional and unintentional.[19]

Paul Weiler, a professor at Harvard Law School, in a meticulous and balanced analysis of comparable worth published in the *Harvard Law Review*, employs a similar institutional analysis, and concludes that the wage gap is more in the range of 10% to 15%, once mitigating factors are considered. Weiler's position is less typical than Treiman and Hartmann's, because his analysis of the wage gap tends to limit his enthusiasm for imposing comparable worth as a requirement on the entire economy.

In assessing the wage gap, Weiler takes into account several factors:

(1) The differences in hours worked between men and women, that is, women work fewer hours then men. But the 60 cents figure is based on full-time work, which the Labor Department considers as all work in excess of 35 hours per week. Thus, part of the disparity in wages is accounted for by women working less overtime than men and less than 40-hour workweeks. When one factors in an estimate of this difference in working hours, the disparity is reduced to 25%. So, this factor alone accounts for 15% of the wage gap.

(2) Women, while enjoying roughly the same educational attainment as men, have less labor force experience and shorter tenures with their current employers. Both factors tend to diminish their wages. Half of the remaining disparity can be accounted for, he contends, by this factor of differences in human capital.

(3) Another factor to be considered, is hazardous or arduous working conditions. Men's work is on average more risky and is performed under unpleasant circumstances, and such jobs receive extra pay to compensate for these qualities.

Weiler concludes that:

> If we take into consideration all three factors that should and do influence earnings—the hours of work on the job, the length of experience in the labor force, and the location, hazards, and other conditions of work—then the maximum level of wage gap to be explained by sex discrimination, and which might thereby be closed by a comparable worth strategy, is on the order of ten to fifteen percent.

Another factor that accounts for part of the wage gap, Weiler says, is too frequently ignored. He calls this factor the "Marriage Gap." Women who have never married have historically received wages roughly comparable to men's. The wage gap, then, is a phenomenon obtaining between men and women who are married.

For men, marriage and the birth of children raises earnings, but for women it is an impediment. "My point is simply that, to the extent that the interaction between marriage and the labor market is the source of the bulk of the gender wage gap, one cannot thereby infer that the jobs predominantly filled by women are inherently undervalued and underpaid."[21]

Thus, Weiler does not endorse the entire baggage of the comparable worth case, but yet he seems to endorse a strategy for achieving pay equity that would include federal legislation to mandate that firms employ the same factors in compensating jobs, that is, that the pay of workers should not be "influenced directly or indirectly by the sex composition of particular jobs."[22] Yet, he is skeptical of enshrining comparable worth as a legal remedy, preferring at this stage to rely on union bargaining for pay equity, government contracts as a carrot to those firms who do employ sex-neutral wage-setting policies, and adding a comparable worth dimension to Executive Order 11246 (the executive order that mandated affirmative action for federal contractors).[23]

Thus, Weiler holds something of an equivocal position on comparable worth: not wholeheartedly endorsing it as a legal remedy within Title VII of the Civil Rights Act, but expressing much sympathy for the goals of pay equity achieved through more moderate, less sweeping means.

Another effort at decomposing the wage gap—one more typical in its conclusions than Weiler's—was conducted by England, Chassie, and McCormack of the University of Texas at Dallas.[24] They use regression analysis to determine whether differences in skills between male and female occupations can explain any part of the wage gap. Virtually none of that gap can be explained away by skill disparities, they conclude. Female occupations "systematically pay less than is predicted by their skill demands."[25] Their research, the authors contend, helps to identify a third form of discrimination—hiring or promotion discrimination and failure to grant equal pay for equal work are the other two forms—that is addressed by comparable worth: that which entails paying higher wages in predominantly male occupations than female occupations despite similarities in the levels of skill required.[26]

For both the political activists and the academic supporters of pay equity, the wage gap looms as the most critical step in their argument in support of comparable worth. If the wage gap proves illusory, then the conclusion that comparable worth is necessary to eliminate the discriminatory animus of the market will crumble. As we saw with Paul Weiler, if the wage gap seems explicable by factors other than discrimination, even an analyst favorably disposed toward comparable worth may embrace less drastic or more piecemeal measures.

Sex Segregation

Another major contention of the supporters of comparable worth is that the U.S. marketplace is sex segregated, that is, that women are cordoned off into a small number of jobs that have been traditionally performed by members of their sex. As evidence for this form of discrimination, they cite the long history of classified adds for employment that designated certain jobs as male and others as female and the pattern of employers hiring women only for certain jobs and excluding them from others, usually the more highly paid and desirable jobs. While such practices have been unlawful since 1964 and the passage of the Civil Rights Act, the lingering effects of past discrimination prevent women today from integrating into male-dominated occupations.

Sex segregation, many argue, can be traced back to our earliest history, when, for example, women who worked in the mills of New England were separated from male workers and paid less. Protective labor legislation of the latter part of the nineteenth century tended to reinforce such practices, with women being prohibited from entering certain indelicate occupations, such as bartending, mining, and the law, and being barred from night or overtime work and from heavy lifting.[27] Labor unions, too, had a deleterious effect on women's advancement. To monopolize the better paying occupations for their male members, unions went along with protective labor legislation for women and children. Unions insisted that women perform "light" work, with the more important jobs reserved for their male members.[28]

In their study, *Women, Work, and Wages*, Treiman and Hartmann cite several disturbing phenomena that have persisted over time as support for their view that women are segregated in the work place. They calculate that in 1970, 44% of white women would have had to switch their occupations for the distribution of white women across occupational groups to be identical to that of white men. Such occupational segregation by sex has persisted through the past several decades, even though segregation by race has diminished substantially.[29]

According to the U.S. Commission on Civil Rights, which they cite, in 1976 the index of occupational segregation between white men and white women stood at 66.1; for black women and white men the figure was even higher, at 69.3. In other words, 66.1% of white women and 69.3% of black women would have had to change occupations for their distribution in the labor market to have resembled that of white men. (The Census Bureau, from which the commission drew its figures, surveyed 400 job categories, and Treiman and Hartmann only eleven, so their segregation indices differ. Both, however, indicate that segregation by sex has remained fairly constant over the past few decades and more substantial than segregation by race, which has tended to diminish.)[30]

They go on to argue that women's work and men's work differs and that women's work is paid less. Furthermore, "the more an occupation is dominated by women the less it pays."[31] After surveying the 499 wage and salary occupations in the 1970 census, they found that "each additional percent female in an occupation results in an average of about $42 less in annual income: overall, 'women's work' pays about $4,000 less per year on the average than 'men's work'."[32]

To explain the persistence of job segregation by sex, they offer an institutional theory. Markets, rather than being perfectly competitive, as neoclassical economics viewed them, are subject to "rigidities and constraints." Principal among these constraints are internal labor markets (meaning that promotions are made from within a company), union agreements, custom, and the segmentation of labor markets into noncompeting groups on the basis of sex, race, and ethnicity.[33] These factors operate to divide the market into largely shielded groups that are not fungible and do not directly compete with each other.

Observable, too, is the tendency of employers to structure men's jobs so they can advance through a career ladder, thus discouraging them from taking their expensive training elsewhere. Women's jobs tend to have shorter career ladders and, hence, be more vulnerable to market exposure.[34] Furthermore, women tend to work in firms with lower pay scales than firms dominated by men.[35]

For these reasons, they conclude for their Committee on Occupational Classification and Analysis, that comparable worth is a strategy well worth considering, although it may not be a panacea for all the problems encountered by women in the work place. For example, it would do nothing to solve the problem of women working in firms with lower pay scales than those employing men.

One explanation for the prevalence of sex segregation in the marketplace is that women are assigned dead-end jobs at the initial hiring stage. Anne Kahl, in a study conducted for the Bureau of Labor Statistics, drew this conclusion after examining statistics on entry-level job placement during 1980 and 1981. She found that white-collar employment for men typically meant a professional or administrative position, while for women it seemed that while-collar meant clerical. Whereas 60% of the women entered white-collar jobs, only one-third of the males did, with men being much more likely to enter better-paying blue-collar jobs. For those women who did enter the blue-collar fields, most (74%) were confined to operative occupations, the lowest paying.[36]

After reviewing this data, Geraldine Ferraro, former congresswoman, Democratic vice presidential candidate, and a firm supporter of comparable worth, drew these conclusions:

> The real problem with the "free-market theory" is that we are not really operating in a free market in which all individuals have equal access to employment opportunities and persons are compensated on the basis of their productivity or the value of their work. Instead, we are operating in a system that systematically excludes women from certain segments of the market and confines them to a narrow range of jobs that, as a class, are undervalued and underpaid.[37]

She dismisses out of hand the argument of pay equity opponents that women may actually choose lower paying jobs for various personal reasons. Opponents often cite the ease of entry and exit to such jobs and the tendency of skills not to erode with frequent periods of absence from the labor market. Another frequently mentioned advantage of such jobs is their relative flexibility, making adjustments to homemaking tasks easier to accommodate.

Ferraro sees two flaws in this contention: (1) Women do not really have the choice of entering most high-paying men's jobs, and, "Whether through socialization or overt discrimination, women are trained, educated, and led to believe that only certain jobs are appropriate to their role in society."[38] (2) But, more importantly, she finds such a claim irrelevant. Women perform jobs that are essential to society. Why should such women—who have invested heavily in developing their skills—be forced to make different occupational choices "because their jobs are undervalued and underpaid?"

Others have argued, in the same vein, that, contrary to the myth propounded by the opponents of comparable worth, the higher the professional level of a job the greater the flexibility in taking time off or setting working hours.[39]

Comparable worth's supporters look at the figures on female concentration in job categories and conclude that something must be radically amiss for this to occur: Medical secretaries are 100% female; legal secretaries, 99.4%; dental assistants, 97.9%; practical nurses, 97.3%; child-care workers, 86.7%.[40] Indeed, over half of women workers labor in occupations that are at least 70% occupied by women; and 80% of women workers are found in the lower end of the job spectrum, in clerical, sales, service, and factory jobs.[41]

For the proponents, such statistics indicate the prevalence of deep-seated discrimination. Those firms that have segregated work forces are not simply responding to market forces, they argue, but rather are taking advantage of the poor alternatives faced by women in the marketplace as the result of discriminatory practices engaged in by other employers.[42]

Undervaluation: Jobs Pay Less Because Women Do Them

During World War II, the National War Labor Board accused General Electric and Westinghouse Electric Corp. of paying women less for performing the same jobs as men who had departed for the front. Despite the contention of the companies that the women were actually less productive, the board concluded that the companies had engaged in unfair discrimination by paying women less for doing comparable work. In the case of Westinghouse, the women were paid 18% to 20% less, while at General Electric, they received 33% less, although the jobs were evaluated similarly on job evaluations.[43] And before the war, during the 1930s, the companies had reserved certain lower-paying job classifications for women.

For advocates of pay equity, these cases stand as paradigms of how the U.S. labor market operated and, to a great extent, still does operate. Men and women tend to find employment in different jobs—the problem of sex segregation that we just outlined—and the jobs of women typically pay less. Furthermore, and this is key, the contention is that the jobs of women pay less precisely because they are performed by women, not for any valid reasons of differences in skills or educational attainment.

There is a psychological component to this claim. Women's work is undervalued because women themselves and the kind of role they play in the family are underappreciated. Since women's nurturing function in the family goes unpaid, as well as all the other tasks she performs in the household, women who enter the labor force come to be seen as worth less than men. Compounding this perception of women as worth less then men is the tendency of women to be segregated in nurturing vocations. The skills needed to be a child-care provider or a registered nurse, the myth goes, are not all that different from the skills of an unpaid mother. Why should her wage equal that of a man who has to acquire "unnatural" skills?

When occupations turn from being male-dominated to female-dominated this undervaluation is seen most conspicuously. For example, when bank tellers were predominantly men, the position was treated as an entry-level gateway into management. Today, when the field has turned to over 94% female, it is a low-paying job with little possibility for advancement. A similar transformation occurred earlier in the century when women replaced men in the secretarial ranks.

The principal evidence for undervaluation cited by proponents of pay equity is the results of job evaluations performed with techniques developed under a comparable-worth methodology. Typical of the results of such studies is the one conducted in the State of Washington, the one that the state failed to implement, leading the American Federation of State, County, and Municipal Employees to file suit.[44] In that study, the disparity between women's and men's jobs that were ranked as equivalent by the job evaluation mechanism averaged 20%.

We have explored the seminal allegations against the U.S. marketplace by comparable worth supporters—that it disadvantages women to the extent of an almost 40% wage disparity with men, that it segregates women into less desirable and less munificently remunerated occupations, and that it undervalues women's work precisely because women do it. Now, let us turn to the remedy for this seemingly intractable condition, that is, intractable given the tools presently at hand: the marketplace's own correction mechanisms; the Equal Pay Act; and Title VII. None of these mechanisms has secured to women equality in the marketplace—therefore, say the comparable worth activists, something more radical must be instituted to transform women's position and rescue her from the status of second-class citizen. Such is comparable worth: and the mechanism both for highlighting the present inequities and correcting them is job evaluations. It is to this tool that we now turn.

Job Evaluations: Theory and Practice

Comparable worth claims to replace the subjective judgments of employers in the marketplace about the value of various jobs with objective judgments fashioned by experts. Since the marketplace is riddled with discrimination—the extent of which may be difficult to precisely pin down, but which is, nevertheless, quite real and undeniable—individual employers cannot be relied upon to remedy past injustices. Even if past offenders were to take their salaries for secretaries, nurses, bank tellers, etc., from the marketplace, they would only perpetuate the past injustices perpetrated by other employers. Thus, something beyond market mechanisms must be employed to determine the objective or intrinsic worth of jobs to employers.

What is of uppermost importance is that the human element in the measurement of job worth must be eliminated; or if that is not possible, which many supporters concede, then it must be limited within the narrowest band of discretion. To pay people for what they do, rather than for what the market says their job is worth, some mechanism must be found for judging the comparability of jobs. This mechanism is the job evaluation.

Job evaluators, professionals, expert in judging the skills and requirements of a whole panoply of jobs, must replace mercurial employers with their personal tastes and prejudices. These experts will supplant such subjective determinations with job factors, awarding points to the components of jobs, and then matching up seemingly disparate jobs based on the similarity of their overall scores.[45]

A typical job evaluation scheme would look like this: First, all jobs within a firm would be described and then rated according to a preselected group of "compensable factors." These factors are typically skill, responsibility, effort, and working conditions. Each factor is then given a weight: say, 30% to skill; 30% to responsibility; 20% to effort; and 20% to working conditions. Finally, a job-worth score is derived for each job by adding up the weighted scores for each factor.

For comparable worth purposes, jobs that receive similar scores are said to deserve similar wages. As many commentators have pointed out—both proponents and opponents—the manner of weighting the factors, to say nothing of the selection of factors themselves and the human judgment of the evaluators, can greatly affect the outcome. If adverse working conditions are weighted at only 10% and skill at 40%, let us say, then the overall score for each of the jobs evaluated will differ from the scheme described above.[46] With this latter weighting system, men's jobs, which tend to score high on adverse working conditions due to their physical demands and often harsh working conditions, will suffer and women's scores will be enhanced.[47]

Implicit in the case for replacing the vagaries of the market in setting wages with job evaluations administered by compensation experts is the presumption that jobs really do have an intrinsic worth, if not to society as a whole, then at least to a particular employer. In much of the popular literature supporting comparable worth, it is the first claim that seems to be assumed. In the more sophisticated analyses of the academic supporters, however, it is more likely that the assumption is only that jobs have an intrinsic worth to specific employers.

Some advocates have even cast doubt on the notion that jobs have an objective worth, but yet they go on to endorse job evaluation techniques, with the reservation about intrinsic worth serving only as a caveat. Emerging from this notion of intrinsic worth is the further assumption that the worth of various jobs can be measured. Thus, there are two critical moves: (1) that jobs have intrinsic worth; and (2) that this worth can be objectively measured.

These two contentions are important, because much of the critics' case against comparable worth hinges on a denial of them. As the debate over comparable worth has matured, many of the academic advocates have responded to the critics by conceding that no perfect way of assessing the worth of jobs yet exists and that all attempts at measurement must embody values. Treiman and Hartmann, for example, express reservations about these two claims:

> . . . we make no judgments regarding the relative value of jobs to employers or to society or the appropriate relationships among the pay rates for various jobs. The concept of intrinsic job worth—whether it exists, on what it should be based, whether there is a just wage—has been a matter of dispute for many centuries. We do not believe that the value—or worth—of jobs can be determined by scientific methods. Hierarchies of job worth are always, as least in part, a reflection of values.[48]

Despite these serious reservations—which on their face would seem to place the authors in opposition to comparable-worth methodology—they go on to say that job evaluations may be appropriate in assessing current practices of particular employers to determine whether their pay scales embody discriminatory elements. Given their doubts, they confined their study to the use of job evaluation plans within individual firms: "because we do not believe that there is a hierarchy of job worth that could or should be applied to the entire economy, we look only at the comparable worth approach as it could be used to adjust the pay rates of jobs within individual firms."[49]

What they concluded—and their work smacks much of its origins as a committee effort, written with the desire to mollify committee members skeptical of comparable worth—is that the current rudimentary stage of development of job evaluation makes "it impossible at the present time to recommend without reservation" their imposition on the entire economy.[50] Given their experimental nature, the committee did not endorse their imposition on employers by regulatory agencies. But they did leave the door open; job evaluation plans when used as the basis for establishing pay rates within a firm can aid in identifying potential wage discrimination, the committee opined.

Three features of job evaluations were identified by the committee as problematical:

(1) job evaluations are "inherently subjective," and the method may embody sex-stereotyping. thus leading to the undervaluation of women's jobs;
(2) the scores received are highly dependent on the choice of compensable factors and the weights assigned to them, and most use market wage rates to establish the factor weights, and so they incorporate the effects of discrimination from the market wages;
(3) many employers use more than one plan in their firms, thus making comparisons between them difficult.

Later in their study, the committee seemed to look more favorably upon comparable-worth methodology, while still voicing reservations about the possibility of an absolute standard:

> Acceptance of a comparable worth approach—the attempt to measure the worth of jobs directly on the basis of their content—does not require an absolute standard by which the value of worth of *all* jobs can be measured. In the judgment of the committee, no such standard exists nor, in our society, is likely to exist. The relative worth of jobs reflects value judgments as to what features of jobs ought to be compensated, and such judgments typically vary from industry to industry, even from firm to firm. Paying jobs according to their worth requires only that whatever characteristics of jobs are regarded as worthy of compensation by an employer should be equally so regarded irrespective of the sex, race, or ethnicity of job incumbents.[51]

Thus one suggestion that the Treiman and Hartmann team developed for eliminating part of the bias problem in current job evaluation techniques is to use the wage rates of jobs held mainly by white men as a standard of "fair" wages.[52] This would avoid the problem of what ought to be the basis of compensation—the value problem—by taking the market rates of that class of individuals who are not subject to discrimination and applying it to presumed victims.

Paul Weiler found this suggestion promising. He, too, worried about the subjectivity of job evaluations and the dependence of the usual techniques upon the marketplace. As job evaluations are usually conducted, evaluators start with a small number of "benchmark" jobs—that is, jobs in the firm that are easily compared with jobs in the external marketplace. From these benchmarks, other jobs are evaluated.

But this presents a problem for a comparable worth theory. If female jobs have been historically underpaid and discriminated against, then using the benchmark technique will simply perpetuate the problem, instead of solving it. Rather, Weiler suggests, a better technique would be to take as benchmarks jobs that are either integrated or distinctively male. Statistical analysis then would be used to try to derive the implicit value to the firm of the relevant factors that compose such benchmark jobs. These sex-neutral factors and weights then would be systematically applied in assessing the firm's female jobs:

> the focus of inquiry would be the implicit economic evaluation that this particular firm placed on, for example, educational credentials versus the risk of injury, insofar as these values were revealed by what the firm paid for such plant jobs as electrician compared to what it paid for the predominantly male administrative or professional jobs, such as engineer. Whatever reward structure one found beneath the entire array of male or integrated jobs could then be used to determine whether the employer was paying the same price for these same factors when they were displayed in identifiably female positions, such as secretary or nurse.[53]

Contrary to the allegations of comparable worth's detractors, then, Weiler thinks comparable worth need not involve a search for the "just price." Rather, it needs only to require that employers apply the same standards in compensating its female workers as it employs in remunerating its male employees.[54]

Other commentators hold fewer reservations about job evaluation methodology. They concede that the customary type of job evaluation is corrupted by its dependence on the marketplace, yet they hope to fashion a more refined technique that will eliminate the bias.

Pierson, Koziara, and Johannesson are representative of this breed. They define comparable worth as existing when the "empirical relationship" between job content and wages is the same for jobs held by women as for men's jobs.[55] They focus on empirical job content, rather than fixing upon benchmark jobs keyed to the market or the characteristics of individual job holders. They acknowledge that the selection of these empirical dimensions is subjective, but they think the selection can be made in a nonarbitrary fashion. They performed a case study using a methodology that first selected job categories that were 75% female, 75% male, and one mixed. They then isolated the specific dimensions of these jobs and studied the way dollars are assigned to these dimensions.

Their study, conducted for a public sector union in a large industrial state, showed that four out of the five female jobs examined were not paid salaries commensurate with equal pay for comparable worth. The salary shortfalls fell in the range of 15% to 20%.

Ronnie Steinberg offers a slightly different explanation of how job evaluations would work in comparable worth studies. She acknowledges that there can be "no absolute standard of comparable worth" because firms differ in their wage structures as a result of many factors, including the types of jobs, unionization, and the characteristics of the industry. Determining worth, then, must involve a mixture of market wages, the perspective of the employer, and, where applicable, the views of the union.[56]

However they might differ as to the details of job-evaluation methodology, comparable worth supporters are all searching for a device that will be free from sex-bias. The external labor market, if it figures in the analysis at all, will have a minimal impact on the setting of salaries within firms. In this way, it is hoped that the effects of discrimination incorporated in the market can be circumvented.

The proponents of such schemes believe that a refined technique of job evaluation will be necessary, but that it will not be a revolutionary departure from the conventional type of job evaluations that have been used within large companies since World War II. Instead, it will be an evolutionary development from these evaluations, and it will seek only to determine whether all jobs within a firm are evaluated equitably.[57] Where traditional job evaluations have failed is in incorporating the bias of the marketplace and the sexual stereotypes that belittle women's work. Such blemishes, the proponents contend, are not irremediable.

Job Evaluations in Practice

The use of job evaluations to make assessments about the comparability of male and female-dominated jobs has been most widespread at the state level, with studies of their employees conducted or contemplated by over half the states. The two firms that dominate in the field are Norman D. Willis and Associates and Hay Associates. Their methodologies are roughly similar, but they do differ in detail. It will be useful to discuss several state studies to get a better feel for how the evaluations are conducted and the kinds of conclusions that are typically reached.

The most famous of these studies were undertaken by Willis and Associates for the State of Washington. It was these two studies, conducted in 1974 and 1976,[58] that led the American Federation of State, County, and Municipal Employees to bring suit against the state for failure to implement the results. *AFSCME v. State of Washington* gave the proponents of comparable worth their most prominent victory in the courts, only to be overturned on appeal.

The Willis technique uses a point factor scheme. Four factors are isolated and then broken down into subordinate factors. These factors are: *Knowledge and skill*, which is subdivided into job knowledge, managerial skills, and interpersonal communications skills; *Mental Demands*, divided into latitude for independent judgment and nature and extent of problem solving; *Accountability*, composed of the freedom to take action and the nature of the impact upon the end result; a fourth factor, *Working conditions*, including physical effort, hazards, and discomfort.[59] is considered for nonmanagerial jobs.

Willis describes his method as evaluating a "job based on facts, not based on conclusions." Instead of taking existing job descriptions as the starting point of inquiry, Willis has five to ten employees in each job classification under study complete questionnaires, thus providing enough information about the job to evaluate it.

Another important component of the process is the establishment of an evaluation committee composed of a balanced mix of women and men from different backgrounds. The third step is to have each member of the committee, plus the consultant as a neutral party, examine the facts for each classification and make an independent evaluation. Consensus is then reached when the committee debates the "inescapable differences" in judgment that initially separate them.

When this evaluation technique was applied in 1974 to fifty jobs occupied at least 70% by women and sixty-two jobs more than 70% male and to virtually all state classifications in Washington in 1976, it showed that female-dominated jobs averaged about 80% of the pay rates for comparably evaluated male-dominated jobs. The following chart compares the 1974 job-worth points in four classifications—two male-dominated and two female-dominated—with the percent female and monthly salaries of the jobs in 1983 (the year the suit was resolved in the district court).[60]

This table shows a pattern repeated throughout the Willis study: that female-dominated jobs evaluated to be worth the same as male jobs are systematically paid less.

Many comparable worth studies have been conducted by Hay Associates, including one for the State of Illinois that was begun in mid-1982 and concluded with a final report in June of the following year.

In 1981, the Illinois Commission on the Status of Women recommended to

TABLE 1.1

	1974 JOB WORTH POINTS					1983 FIGURES	
Job Title	K&S	MD	A	WC	Total	%Fem	MSalary
Licensed Practical Nurse	106	26	35	15	182	87.5	$1114
Correctional Officer	92	23	35	17	167	11.4	1536
Clerk Typist	70	11	13	0	94	96.4	914
Warehouse Worker	61	10	13	10	94	11.7	1334

(Where K&S equals knowledge and skill, MD equals mental demands, A equals accountability, WC equals working conditions, %Fem equals percent female, and MSalary equals monthly salary.)

the Governor and the General Assembly that a comparable worth study of state job classifications be conducted. The legislature, in 1982, funded a pilot job evaluation study "to determine if sex discrimination exists in the classification system."[61] The commission contracted with Hay Associates to assist them in conducting the study. Benchmark jobs were selected, not for purposes of market comparisons, but rather to simplify the study. Twenty-four job classifications out of the total of over 1500 were examined; the jobs selected for study were heavily populated. Twelve classes of male- and twelve of female-dominated jobs were selected, each of which was at least 80% dominated by a particular sex.

A random sample of twelve incumbents from each benchmark job was then selected to be interviewed to discuss the specifications for their jobs. In some cases, incumbents did not show up for the interviews, and, on average, 50% of those selected participated, along with some union classification experts. For the classes in which no incumbents participated, the Bureau of Personnel verified the accuracy of existing job specifications. In this manner, job descriptions were arrived at for each of the positions.

Job content was then evaluated using the Hay Guide Chart-Profile Method of quantitative job content evaluation. This method attributes numerical values to each of four basic components: *Know-how*, as measured by the three dimensions of practical and technical knowledge, comprehension and utilization of management process, and human relations skills; *Problem-solving*, as measured by the thinking demands of the job placed on it by the environment in which thinking takes place and by the thinking challenge presented by the problems to be resolved; *Accountability*, as measured by the job's impact on the end result as determined by freedom to act, whether the impact is direct or indirect, and the magnitude of the specific area on which its impact is most identifiable; and *Working conditions*, in which three factors are taken into account: any extraordinary physical demands required for the performance of the job; the extent of exposure to fumes, extreme temperatures, potential hazards, etc.; and any extraordinary physical effort required.[62]

The study concluded that male-dominated jobs are rewarded with higher salaries than female jobs, regardless of the levels of job complexity as measured by the job evaluation scheme. Fifty-three percent of women earned less than $16,000 per year, while 89% of men earned over that amount. The commission recommended that the state eliminate disparities between the pay of male and female jobs, which "although different in content, require equivalent skill, effort, responsibility and working conditions."

Table 1.1 lists the findings of both the committee and the Hay Associates evaluators for the twenty-four positions.

A number of interesting points should be observed from the table: The first is that the Hay's evaluation and the committee's evaluation differ both as to

TABLE 1.2

Class Title	M/F	Average Monthly Salary	Committee	Hay	Combined Committee And Hay Points
Nurse IV	F	2,104	537 (1)	480 (1)	1017 (1)
Fin. Inst. Exam. III	M	2,376	353 (6)	464 (2)	817 (4)
Accountant V	M	2,470	438 (3)	451 (3)	889 (3)
Nurse III	F	1,794	478 (2)	415 (4)	893 (2)
Pub. Aid Caseworker IV	F	1,622	388 (4)	372 (5)	760 (5)
E.S. Loc. Off. Mgr. I	M	2,010	252 (11)	291 (6)	543 (8)
L.P.N. II	F	1,298	371 (5)	278 (7)	649 (6)
Electrician	M	2,826	274 (8)	274 (8)	548 (7)
Secretary II	F	1,486	288 (7)	245 (9)	533 (9)
Vet. Emp. Rpr. I	M	1,406	262 (9)	245 (10)	507 (10)
Mental Health Tech. II	F	1,135	258 (10)	236 (11)	494 (11)
Accountant I	F	1,426	199 (15)	233 (12)	432 (13)
Automotive Mech.	M	1,681	192 (17)	228 (13)	420 (15)
Secretary I	F	1,293	239 (12)	203 (14)	442 (12)
Correctional Officer	M	1,438	232 (13)	198 (15)	430 (14)
Highway Main. Equip. Oper.	M	1,812	196 (16)	195 (16)	391 (16)
Stationary Eng.	M	2,389	157 (20)	181 (17)	338 (19)
Highway Maint.	M	1,816	178 (18)	171 (18)	349 (18)
Storekeeper II	M	1,432	150 (22)	157 (19)	307 (20)
Clerk-Typist III	F	1,075	207 (14)	144 (20)	351 (17)
Data Input Oper. II	F	1,012	140 (23)	132 (21)	272 (23)
Switchboard Oper. II	F	1,054	153 (21)	126 (22)	279 (22)
Clerk Typist II	F	983	170 (19)	120 (23)	290 (21)
Security Officer I	M	1,178	98 (24)	116 (24)	214 (24)

the points awarded various jobs and the rankings of the jobs. Comparable worth's critics point to such discrepancies as an example of the subjectivity of the job evaluation technique, while comparable worth's supporters tend to view the same facts in a different light. For the supporters, the differences are something to be ironed out in a committee's discussion process or simply combined to get an overall ranking, as the Illinois study did.

Second, the method yields quite noticeable wage gaps between male and female jobs. For one example, take Nurse IV's score (ranked first, with 1017 points) and compare it with that of the most highly ranked male job, Accountant V (ranked third, with 889 points); the nurse received $2104 per month, while the accountant received $2470. In other words, the nurse received $366 less, even though her job was rated 128 points higher.[63] This amounts to a 15% wage gap, without taking into account the higher rating of the nurse's job.

What infuriates comparable worth supporters even more about the discrepancies highlighted by these types of studies is that outside work and work that requires physical labor is more highly rated and that the kind of stress experienced by clerical workers is ignored. Failure to reward the kinds of stress and hardship experienced by female workers makes the salary discrepancies seem smaller than they otherwise would be.

Wherever job evaluations have been employed on the state and local level for purposes of comparable worth assessments, the results have been similar. Women's jobs have been found to congregate at the lower pay grades, to fall short of men's pay usually by about 20%, and to be highly sex-segregated.

Conclusion

As we will see in the next chapter, all of the main contentions of the comparable worth supporters have been challenged by the critics. These contentions are that: the market is riddled with the effects of discrimination against women; that women are conditioned to be subordinate and, therefore, that the sex-segregation evident in the marketplace is the result of societal oppression; and that a substantial wage gap exists between men's and women's jobs, a gap that cannot be completely accounted for by sex-neutral mitigating factors.

Their recommendations for resolving the inequities of the marketplace have also elicited criticism: that jobs have intrinsic worth, or if not some absolutely objective worth, at least some worth to an employer; and that worth can be objectively measured.

Finally, comparable worth's critics challenge the claim of many supporters that comparable worth will not supplant the marketplace, but only modify its inequity toward women.

Notes

1. Donald J. Treiman and Heidi I. Hartmann, eds., *Women, Work, and Wages: Equal Pay for Jobs of Equal Value* (Washington, D.C.: National Academy Press, 1981), p. 9. This report was written by the Committee on Occupational Classification and Analysis, Assembly of Behavioral and Social Sciences, National Research Council. The committee was established in response to requests from the Department of Labor (which wanted an analysis of its occupational classifications, with respect to its *Dictionary of Occupational Titles*) and the Equal Employment Opportunity Commission (which wanted an analysis of the comparable worth concept). The study was commissioned under the Carter Administration.
2. Paula England, "Socioeconomic Explanations of Job Segregation," in Helen Remick, ed., *Comparable Worth & Wage Discrimination* (Philadelphia: Temple University Press, 1984), p. 28.
3. For one who articulates this position see: Ronnie Steinberg, "'A Want of Harmony': Perspectives on Wage Discrimination and Comparable Worth," in Helen Remick, ed. *Comparable Worth & Wage Discrimination*, pp. 3-27.
4. On institutional labor economics see: John T. Dunlop, "The Task of Contemporary Wage Theory," in *New Concepts in Wage Determination*, ed. George Taylor and Frank C. Pierson (New York: McGraw Hill, 1957), pp. 117-206; Arthur Max Ross, *Trade Union Wage Policy* (Berkeley: University of California Press, 1948). And for more recent representatives see: Peter Doeringer and Michael Piore, *Internal Labor Markets and Manpower Analysis* (Lexington, Mass.: Lexington Books, 1971). Doeringer and Piore describe the operation of internal labor markets that are largely determined by custom in their setting of wages and are fairly autonomous from the external labor market. Many comparable worth supporters rely heavily on their analysis of how labor markets operate. For a discussion of these figures, see: Elaine Sorensen, "Equal Pay for Comparable Worth: A Policy For Eliminating the Undervaluation of Women's Work," 18 *Journal of Economic Issues* 465, 467 (1984).
5. "Equal Pay for 'Comparable Worth' Growing as Job Discrimination Issue," *The New York Times*, September 4, 1984, p. 17.
6. For one who argues in this vein, see: James McMartin's comments at the American Psychological Associations's 1986 meeting, as reported in *Fair Employment Practices*, September 18, 1986, p. 111. He contends that female-dominated jobs may receive less pay than male-dominated ones because of "mother-father" archetypes that exist in our collective unconscious. Traditionally female jobs, he argues, have a nurturing component that is associated with the "mother" archetype. Since mothers are unpaid for what they do, women's jobs are judged by survey respondents not to be underpaid, while male jobs are not natural but depend on acquired skills that people think deserve remuneration.
7. Helen Remick, "The Dilemmas of Implementation: The Case of Nursing," in Helen Remick, ed., *Comparable Worth & Wage Discrimination*, pp. 97-98.
8. Id. at 91.
9. Sharon Toffey Shepela and Ann T. Viviano, "Some Psychological Factors Affecting Job Segregation and Wages," in Helen Remick, ed., *Comparable Worth and Wage Discrimination*, p. 47.
10. Id. at 56.

11. Id. at 23.
12. Daphne Greenwood, "The Institutional Inadequacy of the Market in Determining Comparable Worth: Implications for Value Theory," 18 *Journal of Economic Issues* 457, 457 (1984). While sharing some of the same complaints against the market (the wage gap, sex segregation) with the comparable worth proponents, Greenwood seems more sympathetic to other remedies.
13. While it may not have the resonance of the 60 cents battle cry, most estimates place the wage gap at about 64 cents as of 1986. In one study, released by the Council of Economic Advisors in early 1987, the gap was said to have narrowed to 69 cents. Factors cited for the shrinking gap included: longer labor force experience of women; and greater educational attainments. The report minimized the role of discrimination in accounting for the remaining wage gap. See: *Fair Employment Practices*, February 5, 1987, pp. 13-14.
14. One study, by Gordon W. Green Jr., a Census Bureau labor economist, adds another discouraging note to these figures. He claims the gap in average starting salaries has actually widened during the past decade. In 1970, white women earned a starting salary that was 86% of their male colleagues'; in 1980, that percentage declined to 83. As discussed in: George P. Sape, "Coping with Comparable Worth," *Harv. Bus. Rev* 148 (1985).
15. An ever-growing proportion of the work force is populated with women who have children, and often very young children. 63% of all mothers with children under the age of eighteen worked in 1986, compared with only 56.6% in 1980. 50.8% of all women with children under age three worked in 1986, a 1.3% increase over their numbers just a year before; for purposes of comparison, only 42% of these women worked in 1980, and 34% in 1975. As the age of a woman's children increases, she is more likely to be in the work force: thus, for women with children between fourteen and seventeen, 72.2% were working in 1986. As reported in: Report No. USDL 86-345, Bureau of Labor Statistics; summarized in *Fair Employment Practices*, September 4, 1986, p. 107.
16. "The Wage Gap: Myths and Facts," National Committee on Pay Equity, p. 5.
17. See also: Joy Ann Grune and Nancy Reder, "Pay Equity: An Innovative Public Policy Approach to Eliminating Sex-based Wage Discrimination," 12 *Pubic Personnel Management Journal* 395, 396 (1983).
18. Treiman and Hartmann, *Women, Work, and Wages*, pp. 41-42.
19. Id. at 44. See also: Donald J. Treiman, Heidi I. Hartmann, and Patricia A. Roos, "Assessing Pay Discrimination Using National Data," in *Comparable Worth & Wage Discrimination*, 137-154.
20. Paul Weiler, "The Wage of Sex: The Uses and Limits of Comparable Worth," 99 *Harvard L. Rev.* 1728, 1784 (1986).
21. Id. at 1788.
22. Id. at 1764.
23. Id. at 1801-1807.
24. Paula England, Marilyn Chassie, and Linda McCormack, "Skill Demands and Earnings in Female and Male Occupations," 66 *Sociology and Social Research* 147 (1982).
25. Id. at 147.
26. Id. at 164. For more in this vein, see: "Equal Pay, Comparable Work, and Job Evaluation, 90 *Yale Law Journal* 657, 658-662 (1981); Mary Corcoran and Greg Duncan, "Work History, Labor Force Attachment, and Earnings Differences Be-

tween the Races and Sexes," 14 *Journal of Human Resources* 3 (1979); Daphne Greenwood, "Institutional Inadequacy of the Market in Determining Comparable Worth," at 458-460.

27. For arguments of this sort, see: Ellen Matari, Mary Rubin, Karen Sacks, and Catherine R. Selden, "Equal Pay for Work of Comparable Value," 73 *Special Libraries* 108, 109 (1982); Nancy S. Barrett, "The Impact of Public Policy Programs on the Status of Women: Obstacles to Economic Parity for Women," 72 *American Economic Review* 160, 160 (1982). Barrett, however, is no enthusiast of comparable worth, preferring a remedy to sex segregation and unequal pay that would mandate a reform of the American family that would divide the housework equally. She sees comparable worth as stereotyping women.

28. See: Judith Anne Pauley, "The Exception Swallows the Rule: Market Conditions as a 'Factor Other than Sex' in Title VII Disparate Impact Litigation," 86 *West Virginia Law Review* 165, 167 (1983).

29. Treiman and Hartmann, *Women, Work, and Wages*, at 25.

30. Id. at 27-28.

31. Id. at 28.

32. Id.

33. Id. at 44-45.

34. Id. at 49.

35. Id. at 52.

36. Anne Kahl, "Characteristics of Job Entrants in 1980-1981," 27 *Occupational Outlook Quarterly* 18 (1983).

37. Geraldine A. Ferraro, "Bridging the Wage Gap: Pay Equity and Job Evaluations," 39 *American Psychologist* 1166, 1168 (1984).

38. Id.

39. Daphne Greenwood, "The Institutional Inadequacy of the Market in Determining Comparable Worth," at 460. For more on the issue of job segregation in general, see: Ruth G. Blumrosen, "Wage Discrimination, Job Segregation, and Women Workers," 6 *Women's Rights Law Reporter* 19 (1980). Sandra Hurd, Paula A. Murray, and Bill Shaw, "Comparable Worth: A Legal and Ethical Analysis," 22 *American Business Law Journal* 408 (1984). The authors argue that "wage discrimination follows from job segregation." (at 418). Job segregation is not the result of education, choice, skills, objective job evaluations, or fair competition. Rather, it results from cultural bias, which denies women equal treatment.

40. Nancy F. Rytina, "Earnings of Men and Women: A Look at Specific Occupations," 25 *Monthly Labor Review* 25, 31 (1982).

41. Ellen Matari, et. al, "Equal Pay for Work of Comparable Value," at 110.

42. Barbara R. Bergmann and Mary W. Gray, "Economic Models as a Means of Calculating Legal Compensation Claims," in Remick, ed., *Comparable Worth & Wage Discrimination*, p. 156.

43. Treiman and Hartmann, *Women, Work, and Wages* at 57. See also: Mutari, et. al., "Equal Pay for Work of Comparable Value," at 108-109.

44. *AFSCME v. State of Washington*, 578 F. Supp. 846 (1983); 770 F. 2d 1401 (1985).

45. One commentator favorable to comparable worth points out an irony in the adoption by unions and women's groups of job evaluation schemes. Job evaluations, she argues, were originally adopted in the 1930s and 1940s as a management tool for avoiding labor unrest and fighting unionism, and also as a means of discriminating against women. Now, this very tool has been adopted by its victims and turned against management, who now seem much less enamored of job evalua-

tions. Danielle P. Jaussaud, "Can Job Evaluation Systems Help Determine the Comparable Worth of Male and Female Occupations?" 473 *Journal of Economic Issues* 473, 474-476 (1984).

46. For a discussion of this issue, see: Donald J. Treiman, "Effect of Choice of Factors and Factor Weights in Job Evaluation," in H. Remick, ed., *Comparable Worth & Wage Discrimination*, at 80-89.

47. For a careful analysis of job evaluation techniques, see: Lorraine D. Eyde, "Evaluating Job Evaluation: Emerging Research Issues for Comparable Worth Analysis," 12 *Public Personnel Management Journal* 425 (1983); Judy B. Fulghum, "The Newest Balancing Act: A Comparable Worth Study," 63 *Personnel Journal* 32 (1984).

48. Treiman and Hartmann, *Women, Work, and Wages*, at 10. Practitioners, in response to this argument, have conceded the impossibility of eliminating subjective assessments, but proceed to argue that this is not a reason for abandoning job evaluations, since they are preferable and more objective than other wage-setting schemes. For example, three members of the Hay Group—one of the two major players in the comparable worth evaluation field—write:

> It is improbable that we will ever validate a universal job evaluation system in terms acceptable to a scientist. This is for obvious reasons. In job evaluation, we are "measuring" subjective material, which requires human judgment against a human value system, whether the act is performed by committees or computers.

Alvin O. Bellak, Marsh W. Bates, and Daniel M. Glasner, "Job Evaluation: Its Role in the Comparable Worth Debate," 418 *Public Personnel Management Journal* 418, 421 (1983). The authors view job evaluation as a "friend" of comparable worth; that is, it can highlight wage disparities between men and women, but it cannot dictate that they ought to be paid the same for jobs receiving the same scores. Other societal factors need to be considered before that judgment can be made. They look to equal opportunity laws already in place for achieving pay equity, rather than to comparable worth, which they see lacking "such broad acceptance and demonstrable validity to support the changes that the advocates of comparable worth seek." (at 424)

49. Id.
50. Id. at 12.
51. Id. at 70.
52. Id. at 82.
53. Paul Weiler, "The Wages of Sex," at 1768-1769.
54. Weiler waffles quite a bit in his evaluation of comparable worth and its suitability for imposition by law on the economy, concluding in the end that it is premature to mandate comparable worth. Yet, in the midst of his analysis (at 1769), he thinks judges could apply the technique he has just outlined to determine whether a firm has discriminated against its female employees in compensation matters. Judges would have to engage in regression analysis to identify the value judgments underlying an employer's compensation scheme for men, yet this is not all that different from what they already do in Equal Pay Act cases, he thinks. Thus, his position seems to be that, while comparable worth is not an impossible theory to conceptualize or to carry out, it would be premature—where other less extreme remedies are available—to impose it wholesale on the economy *at this time*.
55. David Pierson, Karen Shallcross Koziara, and Russell Johannesson, "A Policy-

Capturing Application in a Union Setting,'' in H. Remick, ed., *Comparable Worth & Wage Discrimination*, p. 121.

56. Ronnie Steinberg, " 'A Want of Harmony,' " at 18-19.
57. Some authorities disagree with this view of what conventional job evaluations in industry seek to accomplish. They contend that such schemes are designed to tell employers what various jobs are worth to them, with no inference that they will have to pay any particular amount to the jobs based on that study. See: Janice R. Bellace, "Comparable Worth: Proving Sex-based Wage Discrimination," 69 *Iowa L. Rev.* 655, 676 (1984).
58. A third study—actually the first of the series—was conducted in 1973, but was confined to salary studies of 242 high-level state employees. The subsequent study conducted in 1974 was the first of its kind in the country to apply job evaluation procedures in assessing differences in pay rates based on sex, for jobs of comparable worth.
59. This description of the Willis method is drawn from a summary of the testimony of Martin Kinney and Norman Willis given at hearings on comparable worth in San Francisco and Sacramento, in *Pay Inequities for Women: Comparable Worth and Other Solutions* (California Commission on the Status of Women, 1983), p. 14. The study summarizes hearings held in 1981 in those two cities and in Los Angeles, Fresno, and Eureka. The hearings were co-sponsored by the commission as well as The Department of Industrial Relations, The Fair Employment and Housing Commission, and the Department of Fair Employment and Housing (all California agencies).
60. The chart is drawn from the 1974 Willis study of job worth in the State of Washington as compared with the 1983 salaries and percent female figures; as reported in Carroll Boone, "The Washington State Comparable Worth Study," Access, A Human Development Corporation (1984).
61. "Pilot Project: A Study of Job Classifications Currently Used by the State of Illinois to Determine if Sex Discrimination Exists in the Classification System," Illinois Commission on the Status of Women (June 1983).
62. Id.
63. Another consulting firm, Arthur Young, conducted a comparable worth study using similar methodology (a point-factor job evaluation system) for the State of Iowa. Its conclusions were roughly similar to the others: that classifications dominated by women are paid less than male classifications; that the pay grade differential between male jobs (over 70%) and female jobs was 6.6; and that the higher the percentage of females in a classification, the more likely the job was to fall in a lower salary grade. They recommended that male jobs should be decreased on average between 0.1 and 0.6 pay grades, and female jobs increased by 1.4 to 2.4 grades. See: Arthur Young: Executive Summary, State of Iowa, Comparable Worth Study.

   The legislature had enacted an act in 1983 establishing a comparable worth policy for state employees, providing for a study, and delaying the implementation of the policy. (H.F. 313, Chapter 170). The act stated that:

> It is the policy of this state that a state department, board, commission, or agency shall not discriminate in compensation for work of comparable worth between jobs held predominantly by women and jobs held predominantly by men. "Comparable worth" means the value of work as measured by the composite of the skill, effort, responsibility, and working conditions normally required in the performance of work. (Section 1)

Later, in 1984, the legislature passed a bill (S.F. 2359) that set the first stage of implementation of the study's findings to begin in January, 1985.

I am indebted to Carol Olson, Senate Republican Staff Research Analyst in Iowa, for providing the documents from which the above account was drawn. In a telephone conversation on December 3, 1986 she stated that the initial study in 1983 was undertaken as a result of *AFSCME v. Washington*. Her opinion was that it was a defensive measure, but that Iowa has a tradition of being at the cutting edge of controversial issues. She did not think there was any impetus in the state to apply comparable worth to the private sector, but that there was some talk of mandating it for local governments.

2

The Case against Comparable Worth

The opponents of comparable worth rely principally upon economic arguments to discredit the concept. The main charges against comparable worth can be stated succinctly: that the market is not inherently discriminatory; that the asserted wage gap of 40% is grossly inflated; that it would be too expensive to implement; that it would disrupt the U.S. economy by increasing inflation, driving up unemployment, and making U.S. products less competitive on world markets; that it would harm women's employment by overpricing their services; that it would hurt blue-collar workers because comparable worth evaluation schemes favor education over manual labor; and, finally, that reading such a standard into current antidiscrimination legislation would penalize employers for wage-setting practices over which they have little control.

The opponents also try to respond to the more theoretical claims of the comparable worth supporters. To the proponents' claim that the market is inherently discriminatory, the opponents respond with a description of the marketplace that is straight out of precisely the neoclassical economics tradition that the comparable worth forces scorn. While the opponents often concede that the market and governmental policy, too, may have in the past served to depress women's wages and opportunities, they tend to view the future in a more halcyon light. If only the market were left to work matters out—perhaps, with the concession that the Equal Pay Act and Title VII of the Civil Rights Act are legitimate and ought to remain in place—women's pay would over time approximate the pay of their male colleagues. Thus, comparable worth, which they see as a radical departure from the United States' free-market heritage, would soon be as unnecessary as it is now undesirable.

To reprise the claims of the comparable worth supporters outlined in the previous chapter, they argue that: (1) the market is inherently discriminatory; (2) that a wage gap exists between women's earnings and men's, with women receiving roughly 60% of the wages of men; (3) that the work place is sex-segregated to the disadvantage of women, with women filling the least desirable jobs with the shortest advancement ladders; and (4) that women's work is undervalued precisely because women perform it.

Their solution is to promote comparable worth; first, in the governmental arena and next throughout the private domain. Comparable worth would be achieved through the use of job evaluation schemes that can both measure the extent of the disadvantage that women suffer in particular firms and indicate the amount of the monetary remedy necessary to eliminate the disparity. For many proponents of comparable worth, the ideal way of achieving it is through judicial interpretation; that is, by the courts reading a comparable worth standard of compensation equity into Title VII of the Civil Rights Act. Other avenues of advancement for comparable worth lie in new federal legislation, state legislation, and, on a less sweeping plane, collective bargaining.

The opponents of comparable worth dissent from each of the four contentions of the proponents, and the opponents then go on to critically examine the chosen instrument of executing comparable worth: job evaluations. Naturally, they oppose both reading a comparable worth remedy into Title VII and enacting federal or state legislation mandating comparable worth. Some, although the minority, are not adverse to reaching comparable worth on a firm-by-firm basis through collective bargaining. It is to a more detailed examination of the arguments of comparable worth's adversaries that we now turn.

The Market: Is It Discriminatory?

For the proponents of comparable worth, wages set by the marketplace embody the discriminatory animus of employers against women. To pay women the prevailing wage rate for a particular occupation is merely to perpetuate this historical impediment under which women suffer. Comparable worth's critics, naturally, have a quite different view of the marketplace. The critics, many of whom are themselves economists, embrace the view of the marketplace prevalent in that profession.

The market serves an essential coordinating function. It takes the innumerable desires of individuals for particular goods and services and matches them to the supply. A market for a particular good clears when, through bargaining, the market settles upon a price at which supply and demand are equal. If, for example, the suppliers of apples ask a price higher than the market-clearing price, apples will go unsold because—at that price—the demand falls short of supply. On a market unburdened by barriers to the free movement of prices, the price will fall until a price is reached at which supply will equal demand. Conversely, if the price initially set by the apple growers is too low, buyers will gobble up the apples quickly, and the sellers will raise the price.

Another important function of a market is to give signals to producers about where they ought to expend their capital and productive energies. If there is a sudden disaster—say, an unseasonal freeze in Florida that wipes out much of the orange crop—the higher price for the remaining oranges will encourage others to enter the market, perhaps by importing more oranges from abroad than usual.

To the comparable worth supporters' claim that nurses' wages are kept low, even though nurses are in short supply, because nurses are hired from foreign countries, their free-market opponents would respond that, rather than counting as an indictment of the market, this state of affairs would indicate its smooth functioning. The fact that employers seek to fill positions at the least cost does not indicate a discriminatory animus against women. Rather, it illustrates the normal way in which markets operate.

The labor market, say the critics, is no different from the market for commodities. As George Hildebrand puts it: "The correct view is that the labor market is a market for labor services, where those services are provided by free human beings who cannot be compelled to supply them for a single instant beyond their willingness to do so."[1] Potential employees bargain with employers to get the highest wage for the services they have to offer. If employer X is willing to pay potential employee Y at a weekly rate of $400, and employee Y would gladly work for $300, then the bargain that they will strike lies somewhere between those two points, depending on the bargaining ability of the two parties. The employer will begin with a deliberately low offer, the worker will respond with a counter-bid at something above $300, and the process will continue until a mutually agreeable figure is arrived at, and the bargain will be struck.

The labor market also provides clues to individuals about how they ought to invest their time and talents in developing marketable skills. Where shortages exist and jobs go unfilled, wages rise, thus encouraging people to acquire the skills necessary to fill those jobs.

What the market does not do is establish the value of jobs or rank jobs in any normative sense based on the wages those jobs receive. The wage one receives is like the prices of potatoes and diamonds; no one assumes that potatoes are less valuable (in the sense of being nutritious and useful to sustain life) than diamonds (which are relatively useless) just because a potato sells for a minute fraction of the price of a diamond.[2] The outcome of market forces at any point in time will not conform to any preconceived hierarchy of the worth of jobs; and the pattern constantly shifts as demand changes and the costs of supplying goods and services change.

Perhaps our values are twisted as a society, and the comparable worth supporters undoubtedly think they are, but the market is not at fault because all it does is mirror the free choices of individuals about how they will spend their limited resources. Thus, the comparable worth forces demand too much from the market if they expect it to somehow validate the skills and attributes that women bring to their jobs. Women, just like men, must subject themselves to the impartial forces of the labor market as it constantly fluctuates to equate supply and demand for particular sorts of labor.

June O' Neill, former program director of the Urban Institute's Policy Research on Women and Families and now a staff member of the U.S. Civil Rights Commission, gives an intriguing example of how the market, free from any hint of discrimination, may reward two seemingly comparable jobs quite differently. She takes two jobs—a Spanish-English translator and a French-English translator—which would, presumably, be rated as identical on a comparable-worth evaluation. Even though all job demands that are typically measured in job evaluations might be nearly identical, the market might reward the jobs very differently. Nondiscriminatory reasons that could account for such a difference might include the fact that the demand for one language exceeded the other and that the supply of one may be greater.

How all of these factors would ultimately resolve themselves into wages for the two jobs is impossible to predict a priori. She seriously doubts that any evaluation scheme could arrive at the market-clearing wage. In contrast, she views the market as an efficient mechanism for processing "the scarcity of talents, the talents of heterogeneous individuals and the demands of business and consumers in arriving at a wage."[3] To adopt comparable worth, O'Neill predicts, would be to disrupt the market by capriciously setting wages. What would result would be unintended shortages and surpluses of workers in different fields, and unemployment.[4]

O'Neill has a ready response to one example frequently given by the comparable worth forces. They question the equity of the market when it rewards zookeepers more highly than child-care providers. Are not our children more valuable to society than zoo animals? This apparent dilemma is revealed to be grounded on a fundamental misunderstanding about what markets do. It misstates the issue. For many people know how to take care of young children, while the number of people with the skills to attend to the needs of wild animals are much smaller. Thus, the zookeepers, due to scarcity of supply, command a higher wage. The market is not passing any judgment on the intrinsic worth of the two occupations.[5]

The free-market critics of comparable worth are not, of course, oblivious to certain factors that make the U.S. economy depart from the ideal market of pure economic theory. Such governmental impediments as minimum wage laws, immigrations laws, and laws empowering unions to establish closed shops, among others, all serve to diminish the natural responsiveness of the market to changing times. To the extent that unions can raise the wages of their members above the market rate by, in effect, monopolizing the pool of labor for particular skills, those who are protected by the unions will benefit at the expense of the nonunionized work force.[6]

Two factors relating to unions had an adverse impact on women's wages and access to traditionally male jobs: unions have an historical legacy of discrimination against women, usually by barring their entry to the union hall, thus preventing them from being hired in lucrative trades; and male occupations, mostly in heavy industry, are heavily unionized while traditionally female occupations until recent times have been predominantly nonunion.

The critics view these phenomena not as cause to indict the market, but rather as examples of how the natural tendency of markets to ameliorate the effects of discrimination over time can be hampered by governmental interferences that benefit the haves at the expense of the have-nots. In marked contrast to the supporters of comparable worth, the opponents wish not to turn to more government action as a cure for whatever discrimination might exist in the marketplace, but to less. In fact, the critics argue, governmental policies are more likely to be discriminatory than the market.

Most often cited as an example of government activity that perpetuates discrimination, is South Africa's system of *apartheid*, with the marketplace in that country serving as one means of undermining state-imposed discrimination. Another frequently mentioned example is the system of segregation practiced in the American South in the late nineteenth century, which was embodied in the laws of the states. Slavery, wherever practiced, has almost always, except in the most primitive times, been enshrined in the laws of governments.[7]

The lesson to be drawn from these examples is that the way of correcting past legislative interferences by the U.S. government, which have served, however unintentionally, to perpetuate discrimination, is not to encumber the economy with a vast, untried, and theoretically dubious proposition such as comparable worth. The preferred course, instead, would be to eliminate these legislative impediments and let the market operate more freely.

Gary Becker's *The Economics of Discrimination* has been enormously influential in shaping the thinking of those who oppose comparable worth.[8] While the book, which was originally published in 1957, was not written with the intention of providing ammunition against comparable worth—which was not really a live policy issue until more than two decades later—the thrust of his argument easily lends itself to such a purpose.

Becker tried to provide a framework for analyzing discrimination in the marketplace because of race, religion, sex, or any other nonpecuniary reason. "Individuals are assumed to act," he hypothesized, "as if they have 'tastes for discrimination,' and these tastes are the most important immediate cause of actual discrimination." Thus, when an employer acts in a discriminatory manner toward an employee, he acts as if he incurs "nonpecuniary, psychic costs of production" by employing him.[9]

Becker formulated the quantitative concept of a "discrimination coefficient" to measure the value placed by an employer (or a consumer, or a fellow employee) upon the nonpecuniary cost of employing a member of a minority group against which he had a "taste" for discrimination." With the aid of this concept he analyzed the extent of discrimination against blacks in the North and the South, concluding that the taste for discrimination in the South was twice as large as in the North.[10]

Of more immediate relevance to the comparable worth debate, Becker found that employer discrimination was less in competitive industries than in monopolistic ones. Another theoretical implication of his theory is that employee discrimination is greater in unionized than in competitive labor markets. [11]

Also significant is his finding that discrimination by any group reduces the discriminators' own incomes as well as the incomes of the disparaged group, although the minority suffers more from the effects of such discrimination than the majority. The significance of this finding is that it contravenes the popular view that those who discriminate are benefited by such behavior, that is, that discrimination is in the self-interest (as self-interest is equated with pecuniary interest) of the majority.[12] Contrary to popular opinion, too, is his conclusion that capitalist employers are not the beneficiaries of discrimination by members of their dominant group.[13]

The critics derive some support and consolation from Becker's analysis, principally his findings that discrimination harms those who discriminate, that discrimination is lower in competitive, nonunion settings than in their opposites, and that discrimination does not maximize the self-interest (i.e., pecuniary interest) of those who practice it.

For the opponents, then, the market is to a great extent self-correcting, because it acts to penalize those who make business decisions in an unbusinesslike way, say by indulging in racial hatred or sexual stereotyping. Over the long run, such businesses will languish while their more meritocratic competitors will prosper. As economist Robert Higgs opines:

> The most effective way to eliminate discrimination is to make all markets as competitive as possible. Competitive markets place costs of discrimination on discriminators far more readily than any other alternatives, certainly far more readily than a political alternative.[14]

In contrast, the establishment of comparable worth would mean that the government and its equal-opportunity regulators would remain forever enmeshed in the work place, supplanting neutral market decisions with their own value judgments. One effect of imposing comparable worth standards rather than the market would be to, in effect, mandate a minimum wage for women's jobs. It would say to employers that for women's jobs x, y, and z, which are judged comparable to men's jobs a, b, and c, you must pay set minimums for each.

Jennifer Roback, an economist at George Mason University, argues that if women's wages were set above the market-clearing wage established in the market, women will suffer the same kind of deleterious consequences as black youths under our current minimum wage laws. While some women will be winners—garnering higher wages for the same job than they would have on the market—others will be losers, when they simply cannot find employment at the artificially inflated, mandated rate. By artificially increasing wages for women's jobs, comparable worth would increase the incentive for women to enter traditionally female occupations and decrease the incentive to experiment with nontraditional jobs. Consequently, it would reinforce stereotypes and intensify the competition for traditionally female jobs.

One unpleasant side effect would be an oversupply of applicants in these traditional jobs. Under such circumstances, employers have a tendency to discriminate on factors other than the ability to do the job and to hire only those with the best credentials. Thus, like black teenagers, who suffer higher unemployment compared with white youths, Roback fears that under a comparable worth scenario college educated women would get the now scarcer traditionally female jobs in preference to older, less educated women reentering the labor force.

Ironically, then, precisely those whom the women's movement wishes to help would suffer under comparable worth.

To make matters even worse, artificially inflated wages for women would encourage employers to substitute capital for labor—technology for secretaries, for example—thus further diminishing the pool of jobs.[15] A far better way to help older and working-class women, Roback believes, is to encourage them to enter nontraditional fields. Comparable worth, she concludes, "exaggerates all the problems the women's movement has been trying to change."[16]

Other critics view the effects of the implementation of comparable worth in even more dire terms. Philosopher Michael Levin, for one, argues that the only alternative to the market is state control, and that comparable worth would entail endless government intervention. As long as individuals are left to enjoy their accustomed economic liberty, wages will be set at the market price; if they are deprived of such freedom, the only remedy is state control.

By implication, then, he sees no middle course, no halfway solutions like comparable worth. To close the wage gap as of 1983, he estimates that it would cost $250 billion, or 15% of the entire wages paid in that year. In the long run, inflating women's salaries would have a disincentive effect on the work of both males and females: women would be getting more without having to work harder; while the men's wages would be held down until the wage gap disappeared. He predicts a "crisis of extreme proportions," should comparable worth be adopted.[17]

According to political scientist Jeremy Rabkin, the implementation of comparable worth would present major difficulties. The theory would be difficult

to limit, that is, it would spread beyond public employment. By logical implication, the theory could not be limited to women or even minorities, but it
would ultimately reach white males and, thus, the entire work force. In the
final analysis, he contends, the theory would be applied to all occupations and
the effect of this on the work force is incalculable.[18]

In summation, then, the critics argue that the marketplace more efficiently
displaces any discrimination against women that might exist than would an
extreme alternative, such as comparable worth. The supporters fundamentally
misunderstand the nature of markets when they think relative wages indicate a
societal judgment about the worth of jobs and the people who perform them.
What the market does is to equate supply and demand; and this is precisely
what comparable worth would fail to do.[19] The result of adopting comparable
worth would be economic chaos, followed by massive state intervention. Unemployment would rise along with inflation, and government regulators
would intrude into 12 million work places, a frightening prospect and one that
would make the burden of regulation lie even heavier on U.S. industry.[20]

The Wage Gap

Comparable worth's detractors have tried to dispute the inference that the
proponents draw from the raw data on the wage gap, i.e., that the wage disparity between the sexes can only be explained by discrimination on the part
of employers.

June O'Neill argues that the 64% wage differential between women's work
and men's is a flawed measure for various reasons. For one, it is based on a
definition of full-time employment as 35 hours or more, thus ignoring the fact
that full-time women work 9% to 10% fewer hours than men. She thinks a
better statistic is hourly earnings in one's present job. On this basis, women in
1983 earned 72% of what men earned. However, as O'Neill points out, this
figure may mask some significant progress. Women in the twenty-to-twenty-
four-year-old age bracket earn 89% of their male peers' earnings.

O'Neill further points out that this gap has narrowed in recent years, with
women in this same age group earning only 81% of the male average salary in
1979. Furthermore, as Thomas Sowell has pointed out, single women between the ages of twenty-five and sixty-four earn 91% of the income of men
who are also single.[21] Single men and single women are more nearly alike in
their earning power than married men and married women.

These phenomena lead O'Neill to speculate that factors other than discrimination account for the disparity in earnings between men and women. She
enumerates several factors that go a long way toward explaining the wage gap
in nondiscriminatory terms. These factors include: (1) the fact that women
have lower investments in schooling; and (2) that women currently employed

have worked 60% of their working lives, while men have worked almost continuously. These two factors alone can explain about half of the remaining earnings differential between the sexes, O'Neill contends.

The impact of these two factors on dissolving such a large portion of the wage gap should be underscored, since both of these reflect choices that women have made, mostly in response to their roles in the family, principally their childbearing and childrearing responsibilities. While the proponents of comparable worth tend to view these factors as the result of societal discrimination and stereotyping of women, it would be difficult to deny that significant numbers of women do make both educational and employment decisions based on their responsibilities within the family.

O'Neill then examined data from the National Longitudinal Survey (begun in 1968) and measured the effect on the wage gap after accounting for the influence of certain measurable factors, including "male-female differences in work experience, job tenure, and schooling, as well as differences in plant size" and other job characteristics, such as years of training required to master a skill, the dangerousness of the occupation, and whether the occupation had a high concentration of women. After taking these factors into account, she concluded that the wage gap had narrowed to 12%.[22]

Is this residual, then, the result of discrimination? O'Neill finds this question impossible to answer because of the difficulty of assessing other, more intangible, qualities that may differentiate female from male workers. Other factors that are difficult to quantify may explain most of the rest of the wage gap: women's expectations are different from men's, particularly in regard to their roles in the family, with women in great numbers assuming that their wages will be the family's secondary income and that they will not be continuously in the work force.[23]

Given these disparate roles in the family, women tend to take different courses in high school and college, courses less directly tied to future employment than those selected by men, and this was particularly true of middle-aged women and older women. Once these choices have been made, for the middle-aged and older, the effect lingers on. But O'Neill is willing to concede that discrimination may account for part of the residual and even that the residual itself might underestimate discrimination if some of the quantifiable factors themselves are affected by discrimination.

As evidence for the contention that women's early expectations affect their present wage levels, she cites the National Longitudinal Study, which asked women between the ages of fourteen and twenty-four the following question: "What do you want to do when you're thirty-five? Do you expect to be predominantly a homemaker, or do your expect to have some kind of career?" While a minority expressed a desire to have a career, by the time the cohort reached the age of thirty-five, nearly 70% of them were employed. Those who intended all along to pursue careers tended to gravitate to math and science courses in school and to male-dominated professions once they graduated, but those who had intended to become homemakers were typically employed in traditionally female jobs. Her conclusion is that expectations are very important in explaining the wage gap, although the extent of their influence is difficult to measure. What is encouraging, though, for the long term is that women's career expectations are changing, and the study revealed growing numbers of women who intend to pursue jobs rather than homemaking. In 1973, 57% of women between twenty-five and twenty-nine expected to work, while in 1978 that figure had risen to 77%.[24]

The persistence of the wage gap since the 1950s is a fact often cited by the comparable worth supporters, with the gap even widening a bit in the mid-1970s. O'Neill thought this puzzling, too, as she found it implausible to suppose that discrimination had intensified over those decades, since such a supposition seemed to be at odds with the observable progress that women have made.

She tried to discover an explanation for the wage gap's seeming intractability. What she discerned was that in the 1950s, women in the work force had 1.6 years more education on average than their male co-workers. As women flooded the marketplace, this profile changed dramatically. The entry of such women into the labor force, women with little job experience and no college education, can more than account for the widening of the wage gap in the 1970s; in more precise terms, this change alone would add 7% to the wage gap. Another 2% would be added by the widening in the gap between male job tenure and female that took place between the early 1950s and the mid-1960s. She discovered, too, that the wage gap for women under thirty-five had narrowed significantly since 1965, a hopeful sign. Over the next decade, she foresees the gap narrowing even further as women's work roles mimic men's, as they invest more in college education, and increase their work experience.[25]

Other critics of comparable worth are equally skeptical of the conclusion of market discrimination that the supporters derive from the wage gap. Jennifer Roback points to the fact that in 1950 there were only 17.8 million women working, but that the figure had risen dramatically by 1982 to 47 million. This increase in supply, naturally, would be associated with a decrease in price, just as the baby boomers' entry into the work force depressed the market for entry-level positions, with those positions commanding 63% of the wages of older workers in 1968 and only 54% in 1974 when many of the boomers came of age. She is particularly skeptical of cross-section studies conducted by the supporters, in which they try to weigh the attributes of male and female jobs, reducing the earning gap by half, and then attribute the residual gap to discrimination. If the same were done for a cross-section of jobs dominated by white males, she argues, only 40% to 50% of the wage gap between comparable positions could be accounted for. She concludes that:

> it seems quite likely that residual earnings disparities are not really an index of discrimination; in fact, the possibility that there is no discrimination whatsoever cannot be ruled out. . . . So it is possible that men and women have widely indifferent amounts of unmeasured characteristics, at least enough so that if they could be measured, there might be no significant wage differential at all. . . . Comparable worth asks policymakers to make precise wage adjustments to correct for a problem of unknown size.[26]

Roback, like O'Neill, finds the similarity in the wages of single males and females quite revealing. The absence from the labor force to bear children has economic consequences and these have nothing to do with discrimination. In the past, women who expected to have children chose occupations with relatively easy movement of skills and skills that do not quickly become obsolete or atrophy. As women's expectations have changed, as households have become more dependent on women's wages—70% of households depended solely on male earnings in 1950, but by 1984 this figure had plunged to 15%—more women have entered male occupations. These women have placed more emphasis upon financial rewards and less on flexibility.[27]

This emphasis on the different roles of men and women in the family and the effect these differences have on the earnings and occupations of women is a frequently voiced refrain among comparable worth's detractors. Brigitte Berger, a sociologist at Wellesley College, points out that women are engaged in a "heroic balancing act" as they try to juggle work and family. Without women's entry into the work place to supplement family income, U.S. families would have experienced a substantial decline in real incomes. The large number of women who are employed part-time indicates the extent of this supplementary role. While in 1981, 62% of married women worked, only 46% of these working women were employed in full-time, year-round jobs. Thus, the majority of married women who worked did so on a part-time bases, a clear indication that, for these women, work was of a supplementary nature.

Berger cites studies that show that women often choose less demanding jobs so they can have the time free to devote to their families. Studies on the income disparities between male and female doctors and lawyers indicate that the differences are not due to discrimination, but rather to women's preferences for working in those subdisciplines that have more restricted time commitments, thus freeing them to devote time to their families. When women without children are compared with men, the gap decreases.[28] The differences in family roles and the effect these have on earnings is succinctly captured by Anna Kondratas:

The pay gap between married men and unmarried men is about the same as between men and women overall. Married men earn far more than unmarried men and married me n with children earn even more than married men without children. There is almost no pay gap between single men and single women. Think about that. Married women, on the other hand, earn far less than single women, and married women with children earn less than married women without. Obviously this reflects not labor market discrimination, but the different roles of men and women in the family.[29]

In the same spirit, another critic, Solomon William Polachek, an economist, identifies differences in family characteristics as of key importance in explaining the wage gap. Being married and having children has an opposite effect on women and men; while these life events depress women's earnings they have exactly the opposite effect on men's.[30] Typically, the opponents wonder why the pay gap between married and unmarried men—which stands at 61% and is larger than the male-female gap—is not also attributed to discrimination by the supporters of comparable worth.

What the comparable worth enthusiasts fail to understand, finally, is that most women choose the occupations they are in; at this late date, they become nurses, secretaries, and teachers because those are the jobs they prefer.[31] Where the opponents see freedom of choice, the advocates of comparable worth see societal oppression, molding of women into stereotypical roles, and discrimination. To the opponents, the comparable worth supporters, by viewing women in this helpless light, do much to undermine their cause.

Now, the comparable worth supporters have rather strong reactions to the derogation of their wage-gap arguments, and, indeed, they must, since the case for comparable worth relies principally upon the wage-gap contention and its interpretation as resulting from discrimination. By this stage of the comparable worth debate, many of the advocates concede that the wage gap is not nearly as large as the 60% rhetoric of the activists would pretend. But whatever residue remains, after statistical analysis accounts for differences between men and women, the proponents still attribute to discrimination.

Also, they view many of the factors that the opponents use to militate against the wage gap as being the result of discrimination—such factors as the level of schooling and duration of work force experience. The family, and women's responsibilities in it, are typically viewed in a much more malign perspective by the supporters. If women are placed at a competitive disadvantage as a result of marriage, this is not a freely chosen lot, but one foisted upon women by an oppressive society. It is society that forces women to take on a disproportionate load of family responsibility, even when she works full-time as does her mate. Liberation from family responsibilities, or at least a fairer sharing of them between husband and wife, would go a long way toward allowing women to compete on a more equal footing with men.

Seemingly so far apart on the wage-gap issue, on closer examination, both sides are not that far apart at all on the facts of the wage gap, at least if one considers only the academics and not the activists. They may differ over percentages, but they concur that the wage gap is something less than the 40% figure popularly quoted. Whether the gap remaining after statistical analysis is 25%, 20%, or only 10% depends on who is doing the statistical manipulation. But what really divides the two camps is what interpretation ought to be placed on the residual: for the supporters of comparable worth the explanation is discrimination; for their adversaries, it is a combination of factors of role differences, tastes and preferences, and other intangibles that are difficult to quantify.

Sex Segregation and Undervaluation

Just as they view the causes of the wage gap much differently than do the supporters of comparable worth, the opponents see the sex-segregation contention as unpersuasive. Again, they point to the investments in human capital that women make when they take courses in school and when they prepare for lives that, until very recently, have been centered about their families.[32] Women's choices—their preferences for jobs with flexibility and easily transferable skills that lend themselves to a balancing of family needs—account for the apparent sex segregation of the work force; discrimination does not, at least not to a very large or measurable extent. What they find particularly disconcerting about comparable worth is that, rather then mitigating the presumed problem of sex segregation, the "remedy" will only exacerbate the situation. Thus, even if the proponents' analysis of the problem were correct, which of course they deny, the solution would only intensify the segregation.

Why is this so? If comparable worth were mandated, women would be encouraged to remain in traditionally female occupations and they would feel less pecuniary pressure toward entering traditionally male fields. Even worse, women would come to see themselves as weaker and dependent upon the state to reward them when they could not succeed on the open market. With the high level of divorce in the country, women need to prepare themselves for new challenges and more lucrative careers, and comparable worth would do nothing to encourage this.

They find equally unpersuasive the supporter's argument that women's work is undervalued because women do it. Frequently cited by the comparable worth forces is the example of secretaries: as the vocation turned from male to female, so the claim goes, the job lost prestige and wages declined. June O'Neill responds that the character of the job changed when women entered the ranks, as it became more routinized and less managerial, thus accounting for the decline. Rather than attributing lower salaries in traditionally female occupations to discrimination, they view it, again, as a result of women's choices. Given her options and her preferences and tastes—her desire to balance family and job—it may very well be rational for her to prefer secretarial work to truck driving or garbage collecting, even though she knows her wages will be less. That is simply one factor that must be weighed in her assessment of job options.

Job Evaluations

Skeptical of the ingredients of the comparable worth proponents' case, the adversaries are equally skeptical of their tool for achieving the remedy: job evaluations. Every assumption of the technique falls under scathing critical attack, from the notion of objective value in jobs to the claim that compensation experts can measure the components of jobs and then compare the totals to arrive at a hierarchy. Comparing apples and oranges is an impossibility, they maintain, despite one critic's unusual experience of having a comparable worth enthusiast whip out a chart that compared the various nutritional attributes of the two fruits, while remaining blithely unaware that those comparisons had nothing at all to do with the relative prices of the two.[33]

The search for an objective measure of job worth they find particularly misdirected. Such an effort harkens back to the Medieval notion of a ''just price,'' departures from which were punishable by one's vocational guild.[34] Later, the classical economists and Marx also mistakenly thought they could find in the labor time embodied in a commodity the true value of the good to society.

Economic science, however, progressed beyond these primitive notions to a subjective theory of value; one that viewed all commodities as receiving the equivalent of their marginal utility to the consumer and all labor as receiving its marginal productivity to the firm. This new-found emphasis on utility (at the marginal or final unit purchased) and productivity (at the marginal contribution of the last worker employed) established the importance of the consumer.

Fluctuations in exchange value of various goods are explicable, under the new theory, by changes in consumers' desires for particular goods. Such changes were difficult to explain on the old labor theory, as was the obvious failure of actual goods to exchange in the market on the basis of the number of hours of labor spent producing them. The new theory, too, emphasized the importance of the demand side of the supply/demand equation, while the labor theory tended to view the supply side as determinative and to do so in a rigid manner. The marginal utility theory, developed at the close of the nineteenth century by Jevons in England, Menger in Austria, and Walras in

France, revolutionized economics, and it remains the accepted theory of value among economists to this day.

Michael Levin illustrates the objection to intrinsic worth with the example of a person who develops a difficult and intricate skill like throwing arrows into the air and catching them with his teeth, yet he must survive on quarters tossed to him by passers-by. His skill is unwanted, even though basketball players receive millions for their seemingly lesser skills. Is this unjust; does it ignore his intrinsic worth? No, says Levin, because the skill is economically worthless if no one is willing to pay for it: "Only someone willing to trade something for the service in question can confer economic worth on it."[35] A good's price has no independent meaning, for it merely reflects the ebb and flow of its performance in the market. In search of this "chimera" of intrinsic value, Levin argues, the comparable worth forces are willing to supplant the market price of labor, and this means they are willing to override the "liberty of exchange, association, and contract expressed by market prices."[36]

Furthermore, any attempt to replace the market process for setting the price of labor with artificial assessments of job worth only invites economic disaster, because supply and demand will still operate, but the process will be perpetually misaligned. Much as it is in a centrally planned economy, shortages of some types of labor and goods and an oversupply of others will wreak havoc on the economy. And the situation might even be worse than in the planned economies, because there will be no centrally controlled plan, as inefficient as that is.

The critics also believe the market, over time, does a pretty good job of comparing jobs by incorporating the value society places on various skills. What people are willing to pay for is the end product, and that willingness gets reflected in the price producers are willing to pay different types of labor.[37] Thus, the quest for an objective way to measure value is a bootless one from the outset. It asks the wrong questions, because it assumes value can be measured objectively and independently of the marketplace; and it cannot (at least it cannot if one wishes to remain in the context of a market system) provide a sufficient substitute for the informational role played by prices in the marketplace.

If the quest for objectivity or intrinsic worth is misguided from the outset, then it is not surprising that the critics find all the steps taken to implement comparable worth defective. Job evaluation, the chosen tool of the proponents for rationalizing the labor market, is seen as riddled with subjectivity and even bias. Instead of using job evaluations as large firms traditionally have used them—that is, as one tool toward achieving internal equity for a whole host of jobs that do not have directly correlating jobs in the marketplace—the comparable worth forces wish to use it as *the tool*.

Where large employers use benchmark jobs to make comparisons directly to prevailing wage rates in their local labor markets, comparable worth intends to entirely ignore the external labor market because it is allegedly contaminated by discrimination.[38] Job evaluations for these large employers are not used in isolation to set wages for non-key jobs; they may be supplemented with different job evaluation techniques and with the need to respond to supply and demand for each type of labor. But comparable worth wishes to rid job evaluation of its very narrow, limited function and to enshrine this unscientific, nonobjective technique into a replacement for the market.

Without the market as a check on the accuracy of a particular job evaluation scheme, the comparable-worth-type job evaluation would be subjective and, hence, arbitrary, depending for its outcome upon the way the study was structured. It would only be the merest of coincidences if two studies produced identical or even similar results. Each expert, employing his own particular techniques, would arrive at different results. Daniel Seligman illustrates this point by citing testimony by two experts in the *AFSCME v. Washington* case.

The state attorney general at trial tried to counter the results of the Willis studies with another expert's testimony. (The Willis studies, commissioned by the state, were the basis of AFSCME's suit. They showed a wide disparity between the wages of female and male-dominated job classifications, a disparity the union alleged that the state had failed to remedy.)

The state's expert, Paul Richard Jeanneret, employing his own job evaluation scheme, produced substantially divergent results, with jobs on average falling 2.9 rankings apart in the two studies. Jeanneret stated that ''in every instance where the Willis method rated a job higher than the PAQ [his system], the job was predominantly female. In every case where the Willis method rated the job lower than the PAQ, the job was exclusively male.''[39] This is a clear example of the disparate results achieved by experts applying their own techniques and biases to the same set of facts.

From the selection of the major and minor factors to be evaluated, to the awarding of points by a committee, to the weighing of the factors, subjectivity is rampant. And what about the selection of a consulting firm to oversee the evaluation, and the choice of committee members to do the evaluating? Here, again, subjectivity runs riot. It is not really remarkable that most participants in comparable worth job evaluations in the states have been individuals committed to the comparable worth notion. Aren't these people biased? Don't they wish to reach conclusions supporting the contention that women have been disadvantaged by the market and should receive pay adjustments? Would not a different set of evaluators, with their own set of values and prejudices, reach very different conclusions?

Brigitte Berger for one, argues that the comparable worth experts are biased, and that they are biased in favor of educational credentials—which are easy to measure—and against the kinds of skills acquired on the job in manual and service vocations. Ironically, while comparable worth professes to benefit women workers, it actually discriminates against the poorest and neediest and in favor of the "white-collar credential jobs." She writes:

> If this comparable worth vision should take hold and become the accepted definition of the value of work in America, a blatant antiworking-class and antiblue-collar work bias will be introduced under the disguise of justice and equality.[40]

Comparable worth, she concludes, is "one of the more aggressively elitist visions of modern life that has surfaced in recent decades."[41]

Richard Burr, a research analyst at the Center for the Study of American Business, has conducted a study comparing the results of comparable worth evaluations in the states. By examining the rankings of the same jobs from one study to the next, he found that the disparities were substantial. To take one example of a secretary, a data entry operator, and a laundry worker, the secretary would be ranked first in Washington and Iowa, but last in Minnesota and Vermont, while the data entry operator would place first in Minnesota but third in Iowa and second in Vermont and Washington. The following table reproduces his results.[42]

In a more extensive comparison of the rankings of jobs in Iowa, Minnesota, and Washington he discovered "vast discrepancies" in the job scores and rankings in these states:

> In Minnesota, for instance, a registered nurse, a chemist, and a social worker all have equal values and would be paid the same. However, Iowa's study finds the nurse worth 29 percent more than the social worker, who in turn is worth 11 percent more than the chemist. While the chemist also receives the lowest point score of the three positions in the Vermont study, the social worker and nurse reverse rankings. The social worker is valued about 10 percent more than the nurse, who is worth 10 percent more than the chemist. H'm.[43]

More curious results emerge, he found, when one compares the scores of the same job across states. Vermont values its photographers twice as highly as Iowa, while Minnesota's photographers are worth 25% more than Iowa's. Burr also found great disagreement about the factors to be evaluated, the

TABLE 2.1
Variations in Job Rankings Across States

	Iowa	Minnesota	Vermont	Washington
Data Entry Operator	3	1	2	2
Laundry Worker I	2	2	1	3
Secretary I	1	3	3	1

weights given to various factors, and the points assigned to each job. In the New Mexico study, four of the eight evaluators could not agree on the level to be assigned to jobs in 824 of the 896 classifications evaluated.

From his study, Burr concludes that "comparable worth is a concept riddled with bias and arbitrariness." The market—"not whimsical committees of lawyers and aggrieved feminists"—is the proper mechanism for setting wages.[44]

Values cannot be eliminated, and to pretend that they can is to abandon rational discourse and claim scientific accuracy, objectivity, where such is inherently impossible. On such slippery grounds of pseudo-scientific objectivity, the comparable worth forces wish to supplant the marketplace with the opinions—for, indeed, that is all they can be—of "experts." But who chooses these experts will determine the outcome. These experts, many of them smitten by comparable worth's allure, will overrule the decisions of millions of individuals exercising their freedom in the marketplace. So, as the opponents see it, you have on the one hand the decisions of so-called experts and, on the other, the free choices of millions of average people: comparable worth or the marketplace?

Given the intractable problems of subjectivity and arbitrariness in the comparable worth methodology, it would be left to legislators, judges, or bureaucrats to determine which "expert's" view ought to be imposed on all of society.[45] Should it be Willis? Or Hays? Or perhaps someone else? Should legislators decree which technique is to constitute comparable worth, or should judges be left to decide that on a case-by-case basis?

If comparable worth were read into Title VII of the Civil Rights Act, as the supporters urge, judges would have to decide between competing expert testimony, using competing methodologies, and arriving at contradictory findings. The complex cases currently litigated under Title VII and the Equal Pay Act would look delightfully simple compared with what judges would be now called upon to decide. This sorry state of affairs would create havoc for employers, as no one would know from day to day whether he was violating equal employment law, and the courts would sink under the burden of cases this uncertainty would generate.

To complicate matters even further: Why, the opponents wonder, will men sit back and watch their relative positions in the wage scale erode? Why won't they demand comparable worth, too, once it had been enshrined in law or by judicial interpretation? Why shouldn't men receive their assessed worth on a job evaluation scheme? Why should they not have a cause of action when they don't receive the same pay as another male-dominated job that received the same number of points? By asking these questions, the critics think they have exposed a slippery slope in comparable worth—that once implemented for women it could not be contained and would soon be imposed on the entire work force. At that stage, the market for wages would be gone; chaos would ensue, followed inexorably by calls for central planning, calls for socialism.

Conclusion

Where the comparable worth enthusiasts see the concept as a cure for the discriminatory animus against women that exists in the marketplace, the opponents see only a radical, if not revolutionary, half-baked scheme to overturn our market economy. The market can live with an Equal Pay Act and even a Title VII, but the critics fear comparable worth is not simply an adjustment to the marketplace to make it more equitable toward minorities. Rather, it is a competing economic system, one more akin to the central planning of the Eastern Bloc, and one likely to produce as chaotic and inequitable an economy as any of those.

Flawed from its inception in the notion that jobs have objective value, comparable worth compounds its initial error by calling for job evaluations freed from market constraints. This sets the supporters adrift in a sea of subjectivity. Since they cannot eliminate values, they seek to replace the values of millions of free individuals expressed every day in the marketplace with the values of job-evaluation experts imbued with feminist ideology. And a misguided feminism at that. The women's movement in its early period in the late 1960s and 70s emphasized women's capacity, women's ability to perform jobs traditionally monopolized by men. Comparable worth sets an entirely different agenda, portraying women in an unflattering light that enshrines their incapacity. Instead of encouraging women to engage in new ventures, it concedes that they will be secretaries, nurses, and teachers for a long time to come and only asks that they be paid more.

As David Kirp and his colleagues observed, in their book *Gender Justice*, the "most significant effect [of comparable worth] would be to perpetuate widespread job segregation":[46] certainly an ironic twist. Sex stereotyping, an early subject of attack by feminists, would only be magnified by comparable worth: another irony.

The critics of comparable worth are not unsympathetic to the frustrations and concerns that underlie many women's support of the movement. They see hope for the improvement in women's position in the marketplace and the eventual erosion of the wage gap in the increased educational attainment of women in recent years, their pursuit of more technical, job-oriented courses, their more long-range commitment to market participation, and their entrance into traditionally male occupations. As for legislation, they see no need for anything beyond what we already have in place—the Equal Pay Act and Title VII—which aim to promote equality of opportunity by making jobs open to all irrespective of sex and by guaranteeing equal pay for equal work.

Notes

1. George H. Hildebrand, "The Market System," in E. Livernash, ed., *Comparable Worth: Issues and Alternatives* (Washington, D.C.: Equal Employment Advisory Council, 1980, 1984), p. 85. He views the labor market as divided into two basic types: the quoted price market and the *bourse*. In the former, the wage is quoted and is not usually subject to negotiation, while, in the latter, the price constantly shifts as supply and demand fluctuate.
2. For an argument of this sort see: June O'Neill, "An Argument for the Marketplace," *Society* 55 (1985). O'Neill writes:

   . . . in product markets we do not require that a pound of soybeans be more expensive than a pound of Belgian chocolates because it is more nutritious, or that the price of water be higher than that of diamonds because it is so much more important to our survival. If asked what the proper scale of prices should be for these products, most people—at least those who have taken Economics I—would give the sensible answer that there is no proper scale—it all depends on the tastes and needs of millions of consumers and the various conditions that determine the costs of production and the supplies of these products. (at 55)

3. Id. at 56.
4. Id. at 55.
5. "Comparable Worth: An Interview with June O'Neill," in *Comparable Worth: Will It Close the Wage Gap?*, 4 *Manhattan Report* 3, 4 (1984).
6. At least for a time. As the current plight of the steel industry and the auto industry attest, when international competition flourishes such inflated prices of labor in those industries spells either the need for wage concessions, plant closings, or failing that, bankruptcy.
7. See: "Discrimination and the Marketplace: An Interview with Robert Higgs," in *Comparable Worth: Will it Close the Pay Gap?*. Higgs argues that discrimination is more prevalent by government officials than by the marketplace because:

   Discrimination in the market often imposes a cost on the discriminator, whereas discrimination by a public official often works just the other way. It may actually provide the public official with a benefit by enhancing his chances of reelection or his popularity with the majority public. (at 9)

8. Gary S. Becker, *The Economics of Discrimination* (Chicago: University of Chicago Press, 1957, 1971). For an example of Becker's influence see: June O'Neill, "Role Differentiation and the Gender Gap in Wage Rates," in L. Larwood, A.H. Stromberg, B.A. Gutek, *Women and Work* (Beverly Hills, CA: Sage, 1985), pp. 64-66.
9. Id. at 153.
10. One finding of Becker's that might count against the freemarket view of the marketplace operating in the long-run to diminish discrimination, is that blacks (or rather, Negroes in the lingo of the 1950s) during the period from 1910 and 1950 had improved their average occupational position in the North and the South, but their position relative to whites has been "remarkably stable." (at 156) He tentatively concluded that the level of discrimination against Negroes had remained relatively stable during those four decades.

11. Id. at 159.
12. Id. at 19.
13. Id. at 21.
14. Higgs, "Discrimination and the Marketplace," at 9.
15. Jennifer Roback, "A Skeptical Feminist Looks at Comparable Worth," 8 *Cato Policy Report* 6, 7 (1986); and *A Matter of Choice* (New York: Priority Press Publications, 1986), pp. 33-38, which Roback wrote for the Twentieth Century Fund. See also: George H. Hildebrand, "The Market System," in E. Robert Livernash, *Comparable Worth: Issues and Alternatives*, p. 84.
16. Roback, *A Matter of Choice*, p. 38.
17. Michael Levin, "Comparable Worth: The Feminist Road to Socialism,": *Commentary* 13, 18 (1984). Levin is a bit more extreme than many of the critics, as he argues that the socialization that the comparable worth supporters deride as oppressive because it fashions little girls for traditional roles is really the result of innate, ineluctable features of the female sex. (at 19) For another prediction of economic chaos should comparable worth be imposed, see: Michael F. Carter, "Comparable Worth: An Idea Whose Time Has Come?," 60 *Personnel Journal* 792, 794 (1981). Carter is a management consultant.
18. Jeremy Rabkin, "Comparable Worth as Civil Rights Policy: Potentials for Disaster," *Comparable Worth: Issue for the 80's*, A Consultation of the U.S. Commission on Civil Rights, Volume 1, pp. 187-195.
19. See: Charles Waldauer, "The Noncomparability of the 'Comparable Worth' Doctrine: An Inappropriate Standard for Determining Sex Discrimination in Pay," 3 *Population Research and Policy Review* 141 (1984). Waldauer attempted to test the comparable worth notion of discrimination in the marketplace by examining the pay scales for academics in higher education. The observed differences in pay between different disciplines were not, he concluded, the result of discrimination, but rather were responses to the opportunity costs facing faculty in terms of the employment opportunities available to them outside the academy. Thus, engineers, scientists, etc. enjoyed higher pay than professors in liberal arts who had few alternatives available to them. In fact, the labor market imbalances in academia are testimony to the fact that external market forces have not been allowed to hold full sway. He concludes from this example that the comparable worth doctrine is economically defective "because it ignores supply factors in labor markets." (at 160)
20. Hildebrand, "The Market System," at 103.
21. Thomas Sowell, *Civil Rights: Rhetoric or Reality* (New York: William Morrow and Co., 1984).
22. June O'Neill, "An Argument Against Comparable Worth," *Comparable Worth: Issue for the 80s*, at 179; and "The Trend in the Male-Female Wage Gap."
23. See: O'Neill, "Role Differentiation and the Gender Gap in Wage Rates," where she argues that fertility and other factors give women a comparative advantage in performing household work. Thus, their role in the family is unlikely to be the result principally of discrimination in the labor market.
24. Id. at 182.
25. June O'Neill, "The Trend in the Male-Female Wage Gap in the United States," 3 *Journal of Labor Economics* S91, S113-115 (1985).
26. Jennifer Roback, *A Matter of Choice*, pp. 28-29.
27. Id. at 30-32.
28. Brigitte Berger, "Comparable Worth at Odds with American Realities," *Comparable Worth: Issue for the 80s*, p. 69. Charles Waldauer mentions another factor

that ought to be considered in explaining the male-female wage gap, and that is the differences in the supply of labor in response to variations in pay. Married women are much less geographically mobile than men; their hours of availability are less flexible; and women tend to be tied to the geographical location of their mates' jobs. Thus, the labor supply of women is less price-sensitive. "The Non-comparability of the 'Comparable Worth' Doctrine: An Inappropriate Standard for Determining Sex Discrimination in Pay," 3 *Population Research and Policy Review* 141, 143-144 (1984).

29. "Comparable Worth: Pay Equity or Social Engineering?" The Heritage Lectures No. 63, February 5, 1986, p. 3.
30. Solomon William Polachek, "Potential Biases in Measuring Male-Female Discrimination." 10 *Journal Human Resources* 205 (1975).
31. Rachel Flick, "The New Feminism and the World of Work," *Public Interest* 33, 43 (1983).
32. On human capital theory as an explanation of apparent sex segregation, see: Solomon William Polachek, "Woman in the Economy: Perspectives on Gender Inequality," *Comparable Worth: Issue for the 80s*, pp. 45-51.
33. Anna Kondratas, "Comparable Worth: Pay Equity or Social Engineering," p. 4.
34. For those who argue in this manner see: Daniel Seligman, " 'Pay Equity' is a Bad Idea," 109 *Fortune* 133, 140 (1984); Hildebrand, "The Market System," at 83; Rita Ricardo-Campbell, *Women and Comparable Worth* (Stanford, CA: Hoover Institution, 1985), p. 2.
35. Levin, "Comparable Worth: The Feminist Road to Socialism," at 16.
36. Id.
37. See for example: Ernest J. McCormick, *Women, Work, and Wages*, Minority Report:

> This relationship between worth and pay, albeit imperfect, is a product of real, impartial forces (as well as of the various possible biases that trouble the committee) and thus cannot rationally be ignored. . . . Stated differently, I am convinced that the comparable worth or value as reflected in the going rates of pay assigned to jobs will over time closely correlate with the underlying hierarchy of values that has evolved in our world of work. . . .[T]his value system is essentially a function of the supply of, and the demand for, individuals who possess the relevant job skills . . . (at 117, 118)

38. See for example: Hildebrand, "The Market System," at 88-89; Waldauer, "The Non-comparability of the 'Comparable Worth' Doctrine," at 142.
39. Daniel Seligman, " 'Pay Equity' is a Bad Idea," at 139.
40. Brigitte Berger, "Comparable Worth at Odds with American Realities," in *Comparable Worth: Issue for the 80s*, p. 71.
41. Id.
42. Richard E. Burr, "Rank Injustice," *Policy Review* 73, 73 (1986). And also: *Are Comparable Worth Systems Truly Comparable?* (St. Louis: Center for the Study of American Business, 1986).
43. Id.
44. For other critics of the subjectivity and arbitrariness of job evaluations see: Clarence Thomas, "Pay Equity and Comparable Worth," 34 *Labor Law Journal* 3, 7 (1983), taken from his testimony before the House Subcommittees on Civil Service, Human Resources, and Compensation Employee Benefits of the Post Office and Civil Service Committee, September 30, 1982; Geoffrey Cowley, "Compa-

rable Worth: Another Terrible Idea," *The Washington Monthly* 52 55-56 (1984); Michael Carter, "Comparable Worth: An Idea Whose Time Has Come," at 793; Kondratas, *Comparable Worth: Pay Equity or Social Engineering?*, pp. 3-4.

45. See for example: Phyllis Schlafly, "Shall I Compare Thee to a Plumber's Pay," *Policy Review* 76, 76 (1985):

> Since it is unlikely that people will agree on allocations of specific numerical points for such imprecise factors as "accountability" and "mental demands," the bottom line is that wages would be fixed by judges or bureaucrats. It's hard to conceive of a more radical attack on the private enterprise system.

46. David Kirp, Mark G. Yudof, and Marlene Strong Franks *Gender Justice* (Chicago: University of Chicago Press, 1986), p. 171.

3

Comparable Worth in the Courts, Federal Government, the States, and Beyond

Comparable worth's supporters have achieved some remarkable successes in advancing their cause. Primarily, these victories have come in the states, with more than half of them conducting comparable worth evaluations of their civil servants and a number of these having already implemented pay-equity adjustments. In Congress, however, the struggle has been noticeably less successful as the Republican-controlled Senate of the Reagan years (up to 1986) succeeded in thwarting House passed legislation calling for a comparable worth evaluation of federal wage scales. The Reagan administration has adamantly opposed comparable worth, and the Justice Department, the U.S. Civil Rights Commission, and the Equal Employment Opportunity Commission (EEOC) have all rejected the concept.

Thus, for the advocates of comparable worth, the courts are a vital battleground. If comparable worth legislation of even the mildest sort—that simply calls for a study but no implementation—cannot pass Congress, then the courts provide another readily available route to attainment. Should comparable worth succeed in the courts, it would go even further than comparable worth bills that have so far passed the House. These bills have only called for studies, not implementation, let alone imposition on the economy beyond the federal bureaucracy. But a comparable worth standard, if interpreted by the courts as a mandate of existing civil rights legislation, would apply universally.

Comparable worth, if it were imposed by the Supreme Court, would circumvent the legislative process and achieve success for the advocates in one sweeping stroke. So far, however, this judicial route to comparable worth has not fulfilled the advocates' expectations, although it has provided enough in the way of sympathetic rulings to keep the dream alive.

In this chapter, we will examine the leading cases that have raised comparable worth as a ground of liability for gender-based wage discrimination, and we will also survey developments in Congress, the federal bureaucracy, and the states. But first, it will be helpful to discuss the key pieces of legislation that have informed the comparable worth debate.

Comparable Worth: The Legislative Framework

Suits that raise a comparable worth theory of liability for wage discrimination seek to extend Title VII of the Civil Rights Act of 1964 beyond the Equal Pay Act's "equal pay for equal work" standard. This effort has proved rather contentious and most courts have not seen fit to make this extension without further legislative guidance. Noticeable, though, have been the decisions, such as that in *AFSCME v. Washington* (1983),[1] which have gone the other way, extending Title VII beyond those instances in which women's jobs can be directly compared[2] with a substantially equal job held by men.

In wage-discrimination litigation, the two pieces of legislation that are most frequently in contention are the Equal Pay Act of 1963 and Title VII of the Civil Rights Act of 1964.[3]

The Equal Pay Act as originally proposed in 1962, and as supported by the Kennedy administration, would have mandated equal pay for "comparable" work; the precise language was "work of comparable character."[4] By a vote of the House, this was changed to the present "equal work" standard. While the legislation passed both houses of Congress in that year, it was not reconciled in conference committee before the end of the 87th Congress, and the act was not finally passed until 1963. The act was justified under the Commerce Clause—the authority given Congress by the Constitution to regulate commerce among the states and with foreign nations—and is now part of the Fair Labor Standards Act of 1938. Among the reasons Congress gave for banning wage differentials based on sex was that such disparities depress wages and living standards, prevent the maximum utilization of the available labor force, promote labor disputes, and constitute an unfair method of competition. The crucial portion of the Act states that:

> (d)(1) No employer having employees subject to any provisions of this section shall discriminate, within any establishment in which such employees are employed, between employees on the basis of sex by paying wages to employees in such establishment at a rate less than the rate at which he pays wages to employees of the opposite sex in such establishment for equal work on jobs the performance of which requires equal skill, effort, and responsibility, and which are performed under similar working conditions, except where such payment is made pursuant to (i) a seniority system; (ii) a merit system; (iii) a system which measures earnings by quantity or quality of production; or (iv) a differential based on any other factor other than sex: *Provided*, That an employer who is paying a wage rate differential in violation of this subsection shall not, in order to comply with the provisions of this subsection, reduce the wage rate of any employee.

The act was fairly narrowly conceived to cover instances in which women were being paid less than men for doing either exactly the same job or substantially the same job. If, for example, a woman performing nursing duties was paid $2 an hour less than a man similarly classified, that would clearly fall within Congress's prohibition. Likewise, if women performing nursing duties were classified as 'nurses' while men performing essentially the same duties were classified as 'medical assistants' and paid $3 an hour more, this too would constitute illegal discrimination.[5]

Congress perceived an injustice—women doing the same jobs as men, yet being paid less by reason of discrimination, whether intentional or not—and prohibited it. It did not go beyond these types of cases where women are doing essentially the same work as men, but being paid less. All sides to the judicial controversy (and the larger controversy) over comparable worth concede this. If expansible language is to be found that could justify comparable worth, it will have to be discerned elsewhere—namely, in Title VII.

Several elements of the Equal Pay Act deserve careful notice.[6] (1) It only applies to workers within an establishment, thus, it cannot be used to make sweeping judgments of equity between different employers (as some more extreme advocates of comparable worth wish to make). (2) It requires an equal work standard, that is, the jobs of men and women, to be compared under this act, must require equal skill, effort, and responsibility, and be performed under similar working conditions.[7] This clearly eliminates the comparisons that comparable worth's supporters wish to make between librarians and truck drivers. (3) It recognizes four defenses to charges of wage discrimination: that the disparity in wages between male and female workers is due to a seniority system, a merit system, a system that measures earnings by quantity or quality of production, or a differential based on any other factor other than sex.[8]

In *Corning Glass Works v. Brennan* (1974),[9] the Supreme Court outlined the procedure for adjudicating Equal Pay Act cases, a procedure the lower courts had been already following. The plaintiff,[10] to carry his or her burden of proof, must show that an employer pays different wages to employees of opposite sexes "on jobs the performance of which required equal skill, effort, and responsibility, and which are performed under similar working conditions." The burden shifts to the employer once the plaintiff has carried his burden of showing that the employer pays workers of one sex more than workers of the other for equal work. The employer must show that the pay disparity is justified under one of the four exceptions noted in the act.[11]

Congress passed the Civil Rights Act in 1964, one year after the Equal Pay Act was enacted. Because the two acts overlap when it comes to banning pay differentials based on sex, much controversy has been generated both in the courts and among commentators about what Congress intended and how the requirements of the two bills ought to be "harmonized." One addition to Title VII of the Civil Rights Act, the title relevant to our subject, has caused the most confusion, and that is the Bennett Amendment, which will be discussed later in this chapter.

The usual problems that courts have in interpreting legislative acts and

Congress' intent is magnified when it comes to Title VII's ban on sex discrimination. Title VII was drafted to prohibit discrimination based on race, color, national origin, and religion; the ban on sex discrimination was appended rather late in the game, indeed, only two days before passage, with no hearings having been conducted on the subject and hardly any floor discussion that could have helped clarify legislative intent. Some commentators have speculated that the whole matter of sexual discrimination was introduced into Title VII by the act's opponents in a last ditch effort to scuttle the legislation.[12]

Title VII has a much broader sweep than the Equal Pay Act; the latter is restricted to a narrow set of circumstances—where jobs are substantially the same—and its purpose is to ensure that men and women doing these jobs are paid equally. Title VII addresses not only concerns about equity in compensation but a whole range of problems generated by societal discrimination: against minorities, ethnic groups, and women.[13]

In addition to issues of compensation, Title VII prohibits discrimination in the terms, conditions, and privileges of employment and bars all attempts to segregate or classify workers based on race, color, religion, sex, or national origin; the heart of Title VII is expressed in the following clauses:

> It shall be an unlawful employment practice for an employer—(1) to fail or refuse to hire or to discharge any individual, or otherwise to discriminate against any individual with respect to his compensation, terms, conditions, or privileges of employment, because of such individual's race, color, religion, sex, or national origin; or (2) limit, segregate, or classify his employees or applicants for employment in any way which would deprive or tend to deprive any individual of employment opportunities or otherwise adversely affect his status as an employee, because of such individual's race, color, religion, sex, or national origin.[14]

After amendments were added to Title VII in 1972, the act now covers all educational institutions, federal, state, and local governments, in addition to the groups covered in the original act (all private employers and labor unions with fifteen or more persons, employment agencies, and joint labor-management committees that provide apprenticeships or training). The act created the Equal Employment Opportunity Commission (EEOC) with regulatory and enforcement powers and mandated that all covered groups must keep detailed records of their compliance efforts. Suits can be filed in the federal district courts either by the EEOC or individual complainants, but the EEOC is first called upon to investigate complaints and try to reach an accommodation with the offending party.

According to EEOC interpretations, for Equal Pay Act purposes, a plaintiff must show only that an employer pays different wages to employees of opposite sexes for equal work; under Title VII, however, a showing needs to be made that the disparity in compensation results from discrimination.[15] Thus, Title VII clearly requires plaintiffs to prove intentional discrimination.

Like Equal Pay Act cases, under Title VII, plaintiffs must establish a prima facie case of discrimination. The burden of rebutting this presumption then shifts to the employer to establish that the action was based on some acceptable, nondiscriminatory reason. The complainant must then try to show that the reason the employer gave was merely pretextual and that the real reason for the action was a discriminatory intent. These cases, especially those that involve class action suits, make elaborate use of statistical evidence, with both plaintiffs and employers marshalling their experts in multivarate regression analysis.[16]

Very often, in compensation disputes, plaintiffs sue under both Title VII and the Equal Pay Act to take advantage of the more liberal damages and attorney's fees provided by Title VII. The relationship between the two acts is a subject of much meditation by the courts.

Another subject of dispute that is particularly relevant to comparable worth cases, is contained in the ensuing clause of Title VII:

> Notwithstanding any other provision of this title, it shall not be an unlawful employment practice for an employer to apply different standards of compensation, or different terms, conditions or privileges of employment pursuant to a bona fide seniority or merit system, or a system which measures earnings by quantity or quality of production or to employees who work in different locations, provided that such differences are not the result of an intention to discriminate because of race, color, religion, sex, or national origin. . . . It shall not be an unlawful employment practice under t his title for any employer to differentiate upon the basis of sex in determining the amount of the wages or compensation paid or to be paid to employees of such employer if such differentiation is authorized by the provisions of Section 6(d) of the Fair Labor Standards Act of 1938 as amended (29 U.S.C. 206(d)).[17]

The first clause was in the original bill, while the latter portion was added as the Bennett Amendment. Now, the original wording, closely, but not precisely, follows the four exceptions allowed in the Equal Pay Act; but now, of course, extended beyond mere compensation disputes to encompass the whole panoply of employee relations.[18] But what does the Bennett Amendment incorporate into Title VII from the Equal Pay Act? Herein lies a genuine puzzle. Does the Bennett Amendment plug into Title VII all of the Equal Pay Act's standards, thus importing the "equal work" standard of the latter? Or does it merely inject the Equal Pay Act's four exceptions (i.e., the affirmative defenses of seniority, merit system, measurements of earnings by quantity or quality of production, or differentials based on any other factor other than sex)?[19]

Now, this may seem a rather arcane debate. Yet, upon its resolution hinges the fate of comparable worth litigation. If Title VII is limited by the "equal work" standard, then comparable worth suits cannot prevail because their rationale is built upon comparisons of jobs that are not similar, but rather, comparable in terms of their worth to the employer. But, alternatively, if the Bennett Amendment merely invokes the four defenses, then Title VII's compensation standard may be more expansive than "equal work," and comparable worth suits have at least a foot in the door. Various judges and commentators have raised a serious problem with the second interpretation of congressional intent: if the Bennett Amendment simply introduced the four defenses from the Equal Pay Act, isn't it simply redundant, that is, doesn't it just replicate the original language in the first clause? If so, its introduction by Senator Bennett becomes inexplicable. Troubling, also, is the lack of congressional debate on whether Title VII should expand the "equal work" standard, especially in the light of Congress's elimination of the "comparable work" language that was in the original version of the Equal Pay Act. We will hear more of this in the next section when we examine some of the leading comparable worth cases.

Suits under the Equal Pay Act or Title VII's prohibition against discrimination in compensation have been brought by individuals, classes, the EEOC, and the Secretary of Labor against private businesses, labor unions, and governmental entities. From a survey of the leading cases, it appears that the most persistently litigious groups are female faculty members of colleges and universities,[20] government employees,[21] nurses,[22] nursing school faculty,[23] female prison guards,[24] female employees of telephone companies,[25] and librarians.[26]

The Equal Pay Act and Title VII provide the legislative background for the comparable worth cases that have reached the courts. As we will see, what the courts have made of these acts and their history in Congress is conflicting and controversial.

In the absence of anything that might pass for a definitive Supreme Court ruling on the issue of whether Title VII of the Civil Rights Act allows for a comparable worth standard of liability, the lower courts have been left to their own devices.

Comparable Worth in the Courts

The Supreme Court decision in *County of Washington v. Gunther* (1981) frames the current debate in the courts on comparable worth. The decision was not a ringing endorsement of the comparable worth concept, nor even a lukewarm endorsement. Rather, the court decided the case narrowly, and it is not clear from this decision exactly what beyond equal pay for equal work Title VII covers.

Thus, the lower federal courts still have been left to their own devices, but now with a vague and interpretable decision by the Supreme Court to wrestle with in making their determinations. In fact, one of the clearest statements in *Gunther* was the court's denial that the decision could be read as an endorsement of comparable worth as a source of liability under Title VII. Many comparable worth supporters, notwithstanding the court's disclaimer, have contended that the court gave its approval to the comparable worth standard. Joy Ann Grune, former Executive Director of the National Committee on Pay Equity, had this to say about *Gunther*:

> The U.S. Supreme Court, in *Gunther v. County of Washington*, has decided that wage discrimination involving jobs that are comparable though not equal is illegal. Such violations of Title VII of the Civil Rights Act must be stopped if women, and the men who work with them in predominantly female jobs, are to be released from employment discrimination.[27]

Such a claim is more the result of enthusiasm for a cause than of a careful reading of the court's decision in *Gunther*, as we shall see.

Before examining the Supreme Court's singular effort at wrestling with a comparable worth-type case in *Gunther*, it will be helpful to examine a few of the pre-*Gunther* decisions by the lower federal courts as they grappled with comparable worth without any superior guidance. These courts were not sympathetic to plaintiffs who raised claims that they were not being compensated fairly by their employers because they performed work in female-dominated job classifications that were in some sense comparable to jobs performed overwhelmingly by men.

In *Christensen v. State of Iowa* (1977),[28] the Eighth Circuit Court of Appeals affirmed the district court ruling against a class of female clerical employees at the University of Northern Iowa. The women entered their appeal under Title VII of the Civil Rights Act, having abandoned their Equal Pay Act claims at the district court level. They contended that the university's practice of paying women in clerical jobs, which are exclusively held by women, less than workers in physical plant jobs, which are predominantly held by men, constituted illegal sex discrimination in compensation. The jobs, they claimed, were of equal value to the university.

The university in 1974 had switched from a method of setting wage scales for nonprofessional employees by reference to wages paid for similar work in the local labor markets to a pay scheme designed by Hayes Associates. Compensation under the Hayes System is set on an "objective evaluation of each job's relative worth to the employer regardless of the market price."[29] The Hayes System evaluated all jobs on the basis of thirty-eight factors, assigning points for each factor and then placing jobs with similar points in the same "labor grade," without respect to the content of the jobs. Then the pay range for each grade was derived by comparing key jobs in the grade to similar positions in the marketplace. Sixteen pay steps were provided in each grade to allow for increased remuneration based on length of service.

But the system proved balky in practice, because the local job market compensated physical plant labor at rates higher than those for clerical duties. The university elevated entry level employees in the physical plant to an advanced step, and so clerical workers were still paid less than the male-dominated physical plant workers, despite their placement in the same labor grade by the Hayes System. The women contended that this practice of paying similarly situated male and female employees differently, despite their equal value to the university—based on the Hayes evaluation—constituted sex discrimination in violation of Title VII.

The clerical workers argued that the higher wages paid to the plant workers was not necessary to attract workers and that this practice merely perpetuated a long history of sex discrimination in the local job market. Furthermore, this discrimination served to pigeon-hole women in a small number of jobs, resulting in an oversupply of workers and depressed wages. The university's reliance in part on prevailing wage rates served only to carry over to the university the tainted wage policies of the marketplace.

The women sought an interpretation of Title VII "that may establish a *prima facie* violation of that Act whenever employees of different sexes receive disparate compensation for work of differing skills that may, subjectively, be of equal value to the employer, but does not command an equal price in the labor market."

The university disputed these points, arguing that by adopting the Hayes System it sought to remove wage inequities between male and female-dominated jobs, but that a complete endorsement of this system became unworkable for some physical plant jobs because they commanded a higher pay scale in the surrounding community than Hayes judged their worth to be to the university. To fill these positions, the university had to pay prevailing rates.

The two sides disputed the interpretation of the Bennett Amendment to Title VII. The university argued, and the district court concurred, that the women did not establish entitlement to relief under Title VII because they failed to demonstrate that work performed by them was "substantially similar" to work performed by the plant employees. Thus, the university embraced a wide interpretation of the Bennett Amendment as incorporating more than the affirmative defenses from the Equal Pay Act; that "more" being the "equal work" standard. The clerical workers hewed to the narrow interpretation of the amendment, the interpretation favorable to comparable worth claims: that the amendment places no such narrow reading on sex discrimination in compensation suits under Title VII.

The appeals court did not resolve this Bennett Amendment conflict, for it concluded that the appellants had failed to make a *prima facie* case; that is, they failed to carry their burden of proof that the differences in wages were based on sex discrimination. The university did not discriminate between male and female employees in the plant jobs; jobs were advertised and open to both sexes without distinction; and women were not locked in clerical jobs by any policy of the university.

The court rejected the women's argument that by adopting marketplace wage rates the university perpetuated sex discrimination. It held that this argument misconstrues the purposes of Title VII, which the court saw as entitling individuals to "equal *opportunities*"—in other words, to equality of employment opportunities and to the elimination of "those discriminatory practices and devices which have fostered racially stratified job environments to the disadvantage of minority citizens."[30]

As the court saw it, the appellants here wished something different and beyond equal opportunity when they saw a violation of Title VII in different wage rates for men and women performing dissimilar jobs that may "subjectively, be of equal value to the employer." The court also looked askance upon the economic theory implicit in the women's contention of market-based wage discrimination:

> Appellants' theory ignores economic realities. The value of the job to the employer represents but one factor affecting wages. Other factors may include the supply of workers willing to do the job and the ability of the workers to band together to bargain collectively for higher wages. We find nothing in the text and history of Title VII suggesting that Congress intended to abrogate the laws of supply and demand or other economic principles that determine wage rates for various kinds of work. We do not interpret Title VII as requiring an employer to ignore the market in setting wage rates for genuinely different work classifications.[31]

This rejection of comparable worth claims on the basis that Congress did not intend to abrogate the market is echoed in another leading case of the pre-*Gunther* period, *Lemons v. City and County of Denver* (1978).[32] Here, nurses working for the city objected to the scheme by which salaries were set for municipal employees. The city established hundreds of job classifications, defined by written descriptions. From these, certain "key classes" of jobs were selected for their ready comparability to similar jobs in the local labor market.

Now, the nurses objected to the comparison of their "key" jobs to nurses in the community. As is typical of the complaints in comparable-worth cases, the nurses maintained that historically nurses have been underpaid because their work has not been properly recognized as a result of the nursing profession's dominance by women. By simply mirroring prevailing wage rates in the nursing profession in the community, they argued, the city perpetuated the existing discrimination. They wished to be placed in a different classification—"General Administrative Series"—so they would be compared to nonnursing positions.

The nurses brought suit under Title VII, the Fourteenth Amendment's equal protection clause, and the Civil Rights Act of 1871.[33] They expressly abandoned any claim under the Equal Pay Act. The district court judge who decided *Lemons*, and who was upheld by the Tenth Circuit Court of Appeals, presented the most interesting decision in this case, and he relied heavily on the Eighth Circuit's decision in *Christensen v. Iowa*.

Chief Judge Winner's oral decision seems to have been generated by a good deal of frustration with the comparable worth concept itself and with the uncertain state of legal interpretation of Title VII. He began his analysis by acknowledging that the case is one of substantial importance. "[I]t is a case," he said, "which is pregnant with the possibility of disrupting the entire economic system of the United States of America."[34]

For the chief judge, it was self-evident why the nurses abandoned any claim under the Equal Play Act, for the very theory of their case was that the city did not discriminate among its employees, but merely mirrored the discrimination in the community that had been passed down through the centuries. While this complaint would not fall within the purview of the Equal Pay Act, because it would not satisfy the single establishment requirement of the act, the plaintiffs argued that it was the type of discrimination that Congress intended to prohibit under Title VII. As the plaintiffs saw it, Congress intended for the courts to undo the historical disadvantage suffered by women. But Chief Judge Winner thought otherwise:

> . . . what we are confronted with here today is history. We're confronted with a history which I have no hesitancy at all in finding has discriminated unfairly and improperly against women. But Congress did not, in my judgment, decide that we were going to roll aside all history and that the Federal Courts should take over the job of leveling out centuries of discrimination. One can go to the Bible and find countless examples of discrimination. To me, the terrifying picture that would be painted if Courts were [to] get into this situation was best exemplified by Dr. Bardwell [one of the expert witnesses] in response to a question or two I asked him.

> I asked him to accept the assumption, which I believed to be true, that secretaries for the last 70 years have been predominantly female, that secretaries by and large are better trained and more highly skilled than salesmen, and that salesmen are predominantly male. But salesmen make more money. And I asked him if he thought that was sexual discrimination. He said that he did, and that corporations should have to pay secretaries more than salesmen.

> So what he is saying is that I should open the Pandora's Box in this case of restructuring the entire economy of the United States of America. I am not going to do it. Some higher Court is going to have to take that step. I don't know how you would ever live with such a program.[35]

The judge then went on to remark that he could not believe Congress intended to mandate that the jobs of all individuals be compared and new pay scales set up by "some group of experts or pseudo experts" who could never agree about anything, anyway. For good measure, he warned any Congress so inclined to contemplate the prospect of facing organized labor with such a scheme:

> I know that if the Court were to order an increase in the pay of the unorganized group, the next round of labor negotiations would use that as a jumping off place. The Courts of this country would be deluged with that type of litigation, and there isn't a Judge in the United States, especially this Judge, qualified to set everybody else's pay. It would be an absolutely hopeless morass.[36]

The laws of economics were very much on the judge's mind. He remarked that even Congress cannot repeal the laws of supply and demand. The supply of nurses is large, compared with the demand, and consequently nurses are paid less. If there is any discrimination in this situation, it lies with professions other than nurses that have historically barred the entry of women. The city, however, presented no such barriers, and so is blameless. It is much "fairer," the judge thought, to pay nurses prevailing rates in the community than for a court to try to make comparisons between nurses and real estate appraisers. Such an attempt would lead to "absolute chaos in the economy."

The chief judge concluded his opinion by rejecting all the claims of the plaintiffs and, for good measure, denying that they had stated any claim under the Equal Pay Act. He warned that any restructuring of the economy along the lines that the nurses desired would be damaging to the country and destructive to our freedom:

> If we are to have, in this country, the legendary 1984 as expressed in the book, the Big Brother looking over our shoulder who is going to dictate our day-to-day ways of life, it's going to have to come from the Congress. It's not going to come, at least, from this Court.[37]

The points made by Chief Judge Winner, although certainly more graphic and heartfelt than in the usual run of court decisions, capture the prevailing attitude of courts to the comparable worth concept prior to *Gunther*.[38] Comparable worth seemed an idea destined to disrupt the U.S. economy by imposing alien, egalitarian ideals upon our market system, by requiring courts to sit as arbitrators of all salaries or at least all salaries within an enterprise, and by forcing employers and judges to rely on "experts" to reconfigure the salary structure of the country.

Judges were skeptical, too, of the contention by the comparable worth supporters that Title VII mandated comparable worth, and they were reluctant to go beyond the Equal Pay Act's "equal work" standard without either instructions from above—i.e., the Supreme Court—or further action by Congress.

In three circuits, however, judges seemed to be more amenable to extending Title VII protection against wage disparities to cases that would not fit the Equal Pay Act's stringent "equal work" requirement. None of these cases presents claims that would go nearly as far as the comparable worth supporters would like: that is, they did not compare job categories as disparate as secretaries and maintenance men. In *Fitzgerald v. Sirloin Stockade* (1980),[39] the plaintiff, a former employee of the company, claimed that she assumed almost all of the duties of her supervisor when he resigned, but that she did not receive his title or the pay he earned as director of the advertising department. She sued under Title VII, alleging discrimination against her throughout her employment because of her sex. The district court concurred, as did the Tenth Circuit appeals court.

The appeals court determined that on the compensation issue, although it did not fall within the "equal work" standard, because she did not perform the same job as her predecessor, the company's discriminatory behavior could, nevertheless, violate Title VII. Their finding, they concluded, does not offend the Bennett Amendment nor the Equal Pay Act standards.

Gunther v. County of Washington (1979)[40] (the case that would eventually reach the Supreme Court), heard by the Ninth Circuit Court of Appeals, also allowed that Title VII could be broader than the Equal Pay Act. Here, the case involved female jail matrons who guarded inmates in the female section of the county jail. Male guards received a higher rate of compensation for guarding inmates in the male section of the jail.

The plaintiffs alleged that they were denied equal pay for equal work, but the district court found that the two sets of jobs were not substantially equal and dismissed the action. On appeal, the plaintiffs continued to argue that they were denied equal pay for work substantially equal to the men's, but also, that even if the work were not substantially equal, at least some of that difference could be attributed to sex discrimination. The appeals court agreed with the district court that the work was not substantially equal, but their inquiry did not end there. They concluded:

> In summary, we hold that, although decisions interpreting the Equal Pay Act are authoritative where plaintiffs suing under Title VII raise a claim of equal pay, plaintiffs are not precluded from suing under Title VII to protest other discriminatory compensation practices unless the practices are authorized under one of the four affirmative defenses contained in the Equal Pay Act and incorporated into Title VII by Section 703(h).[41]

Thus, the court embraced the narrow interpretation of the Bennett Amendment, i.e., that the amendment merely incorporated the four affirmative defenses.

The pre-*Gunther* case that most nearly approached the comparable worth ideal of comparing diverse jobs is one decided by the Third Circuit in 1980: *International Union of Electrical, Radio and Machine Workers (IUE) v. Westinghouse Electric Corp..*[42] But here, the plaintiffs argued that the company set wages for different classifications based on sexual discrimination.

The company had established in the late 1930s a wage system that explicitly placed female job categories in factory jobs on a lower scale then men's, even though they were judged on a point system to be equivalent. In 1965, the company established a unified grading system with no explicit designation of some jobs as men's and others as women's. Yet, 85% of the women were assigned to the lowest four grades. The plaintiffs contended that this system was tainted by residues of the 1930s grading system.

The court held that, if proven, such activity would constitute a violation of Title VII, despite the fact that the jobs held predominantly by women were not the same as the jobs held by men. The court, thus, embraced the narrow view of the Bennett Amendment, arguing that where intentional discrimination is proven, Title VII provides wider protection to women than the Equal Pay Act. The court's majority felt that it would be ironic if Title VII gave less protection against discrimination in wages to females than to racial or religious minorities.

Even in this case, the court did not endorse under Title VII comparisons of jobs as diverse as nurses and real estate appraisers. Rather, what was involved were factory jobs, where women had been clearly assigned to a specific group of jobs, been kept from jobs held by men, and had been paid less. (The women held jobs such as assembly line, subassembly line, and quality control, while the men were janitors, forklift operators, warehousemen, material handlers, and craftsmen.)

In summary, then, the pre-*Gunther* decisions were not terribly encouraging to comparable worth enthusiasts, with most courts shunning such as beyond their legislative mandate, and some castigating the theory as anathema to our market system. Even those cases that could be read as encouraging, merely widened the purview of Title VII beyond the "equal work" standard of the Equal Pay Act, while comparing jobs that were not all that dissimilar.

The Supreme Court Enters the Fray

County of Washington v. Gunther[43] reached the Supreme Court in 1981, and a deeply divided Court on a five-to-four decision would give some guidance to the lower courts, and also some inspiration to the advocates of comparable worth. But the guidance would be of a minimal and ambiguous sort.[44]

As we recall from the previous discussion of *Gunther* at the appeals court level, the case involved female guards who alleged that they were paid less than male guards doing substantially equal work, or, alternatively, that as a result of intentional discrimination their pay was less than that of the male guards. The female guards contended that, as a result of this intentional discrimination, their pay had been set lower than that indicated by the county's own survey of prevailing wage rates in the surrounding marketplace and the worth of their jobs, even though the jobs of men had not been so treated.

The district court had concluded that the jobs of the female guards were not substantially equal to those of the male guards, since the men guarded more than ten times as many prisoners per guard as did the women, and that they were not entitled to equal pay. The appeals court affirmed this conclusion, and the women did not seek review on this claim. Thus, the Supreme Court was limited to a ruling on the claim that, by reason of intentional discrimination, they were paid less than male guards. This was a claim the district court had held to be precluded by the Bennett Amendment, but with which the appeals court disagreed.

Justice Brennan, writing for four of his colleagues (White, Marshall, Blackmun, and Stevens), began his analysis of the issue on a cautionary note:

> We emphasize at the outset the narrowness of the question before us in this case. Respondents' [the female guards'] claim is *not based on the controversial concept of "comparable worth,"* under which plaintiffs might claim increased compensation on the basis of a comparison of the intrinsic worth or difficulty of their job with that of other jobs in the same organization or community. Rather, respondents seek to prove, by direct evidence, that their wages were depressed because of intentional sex discrimination, consisting of setting the wage scale for female guards but not for male guards, at a level lower than its own survey of outside markets and the worth of the jobs warranted. The narrow question in this case is whether such a claim is precluded by the last sentence of SS 703(h) of Title VII, called the "Bennett Amendment."[45] (emphasis added)

Thus, the majority saw itself as deciding on the narrowest of issues, namely, whether the female guards' failure to satisfy the equal work standard of the Equal Pay Act should preclude them from proceeding under Title VII.[46] And the court concluded, as the appeals court had, that "the language of the Bennett Amendment suggests an intention to incorporate only the affirmative defenses of the Equal Pay Act into Title VII."

Justice Brennan did concede that the "language and legislative history of the provision are not unambiguous."[47] He argued that the language of the Bennett Amendment bars sex-based wage discrimination claims under Title VII where the pay differential is "authorized" by the Equal Pay Act. "Authorized" cannot refer to the first part of the act—which prohibits employers from paying males and females at different rates for equal work—but must refer merely to the affirmative defenses in the second part—that exceptions are permitted for seniority systems, merit systems, quantity or quality or production or "any other factor other than sex."

The majority rejected the county's argument that such an interpretation would render the Bennett Amendment superfluous, as the first three of the exceptions were already embodied in section 703(h) before the amendment was appended. Rather, they viewed the amendment as a technical correction designed to ensure that, with respect to the first three exceptions, courts would interpret the standards in the same manner for both Title VII and Equal Pay Act purposes.

What particularly troubled Justice Brennan and his colleagues was that, under the broad interpretation of the Bennett Amendment advocated by the County of Washington, whole classes of women could be subject to wage discrimination and have no remedy under Title VII:

> . . . this means that a woman who is discriminatorily underpaid could obtain no relief—no matter how egregious the discrimination might be—unless her employer also employed a man in an equal job in the same establishment, at a higher rate of pay. Thus, if an employer hired a woman for a unique position in the company and then admitted that her salary would have been higher had she been male, the woman would be unable to obtain legal redress under petitioners' interpretation.[48]

While the county held out the specter of female plaintiffs drawing "any type of comparison imaginable" between male and female-dominated jobs with respect to duties and pay, the majority of the court saw no such specter implicit in this particular case. Such claims would be "manifestly different" from the kind embodied in this case, they concluded. For the women claimed, here, that the county evaluated the worth of their jobs as 90% of that of the male guards, yet paid them only 70% as much, and that the failure of the county to pay them the full evaluated worth of their jobs can be proved to result from intentional sex discrimination. Thus:

> . . . respondent's suit does not require a court to make its own subjective assessment of the value of the male and female guard jobs, or to attempt by statistical technique or other method to quantify the effect of sex discrimination on the wage rates.[49]

The opinion concluded with the concession that the majority had not defined the "precise contours of lawsuits challenging sex discrimination in compensation under Title VII."[50] But what they did decide was that, given this type of claim, it was not barred by the Bennett Amendment to Title VII merely because the female guards do not perform work equal to that of the male guards.

Now, one might wonder where this leaves us. That is not altogether clear. The decision did not endorse comparable worth comparisons of a sweeping sort, nor did it endorse the concept in any explicit way; in fact it did the opposite. Nevertheless, it did open a window to claims under Title VII for wage disparities that go beyond the "equal work" requirement. But how far beyond? That is what the judges declined to decree.

What we can conclude, safely, is that for cases presenting situations of a similar sort to *Gunther*, Title VII will provide a remedy if sexual discrimination is proven as the motivating force behind the pay disparities between male and female jobs. The key ingredients presented by the women guards, as the court saw them, seem to be: (1) that the employer engaged in an evaluative study and then ignored its conclusions with respect to the women and paid them less then male guards; (2) that the jobs, although not identical nor "substantially equal," are not widely dissimilar, but fairly similar for purposes of comparison; and (3) that the pay disparity is alleged to have resulted from sex-discrimination and not some other permissible reason.[51]

Justice Rehnquist for the four dissenters (Chief Justice Burger and Justices Stewart and Powell) mounted a lengthy and spirited dissent. The majority's contention that their ruling was a narrow one did not placate Justice Rehnquist, who argued that even such a narrow ruling would be inconsistent with the legislative history of Title VII and the Equal Pay Act. On his view, there can be no Title VII claim of sex-based wage discrimination without proof of "equal work."

What Justice Rehnquist perceived in the majority's decision was a clear example of the court ignoring traditional canons of statutory construction and relevant legislative history, and, instead, imposing its "unshakable belief that any other result would be unsound public policy."[52]

Regarding the canons of statutory construction, Rehnquist argued that the court disregarded its long-stated rule that "where there is no clear intention otherwise, a specific statute will not be controlled or nullified by a general one, regardless of the priority of enactment."[53] But, under this rule, the Equal Pay Act—a narrowly focused statute—would control Title VII wage-discrimination suits, for the latter is the more general statute.

On legislative history, Rehnquist found clear congressional intent in the debate over the Equal Pay Act to abandon a comparable work standard and replace it with equal work, and he found nothing in the record to indicate that Congress in the very next year reversed its intention. What little legislative comment there was at the time about wage-discrimination under Title VII indicated to him that Congress intended to incorporate the earlier act's equal work standard. Thus, he finds most plausible the broad interpretation of the Bennett Amendment to Title VII, incorporating the equal work standard.

The only saving grace Rehnquist can discern in the court's decision is that it was drawn on such narrow grounds that, "One has the sense that the decision today will be treated like a restricted railroad ticket, 'good for this day and train only.' "[54] He found cause for some relief, one suspects, in the fact that the Court did not endorse comparable worth and that it related without criticizing the county's contention that *Lemons*—the case rejecting a comparison between nurses and dissimilar jobs in the community—is distinguishable. In other words, for Rehnquist the Court could have done a lot more damage, but it did do some.

Comparable Worth in the Courts after Gunther's "Guidance"

Perhaps Justice Rehnquist's prediction that *Gunther* would provide little inspiration for the lower courts to extend Title VII beyond the "equal work" standard was only a bit too halcyon. While most courts have wrestled mightily trying to understand and apply the court's decision in *Gunther*, there has not been a real change of heart on the true comparable worth claims. Title VII, indeed, has been stretched to embrace something more than "equal work" but judges are not clear about how much more.

In one case, however, *Gunther* provided a district court judge with the ammunition he needed to advance the comparable worth cause. That case is the renowned *American Federation of State, County, and Municipal Employees (AFSCME) v. State of Washington.*[55] While the decision was ultimately overturned on appeal, almost two years intervened between the two decisions, years in which the comparable worth forces gained considerable momentum.

Two unions—AFSCME and the Washington Federation of State Employees—filed suit in July 1982 on behalf of 15,500 employees of the State of Washington who held jobs in classifications that were at least 70% filled by females. They claimed, under Title VII, that the state was guilty of sex-based wage discrimination. At the prompting of the Washington Federation of State Employees, the state began in 1974 to study whether the state paid lower wages to women than to men. The two boards that operate the civil service system in Washington concluded that "There are clear indications of pay differences between classes predominately held by men and those predominately held by women within the State systems."[56] They went on to state that such differences are not due solely to job "worth," and they recommended that further study was necessary to determine the amount of the salary disparities.

Governor Evans then contracted with an outside consulting firm, Norman Willis & Associates, one of the leading specialists in comparable worth-type job evaluation studies. The study, conducted in 1974, examined 89 predominately male classifications and compared them with 62 predominately female classifications, predominately being defined by the 70% criterion. The Willis team performed a typical comparable worth study. Using trained evaluation committees, the job classifications were evaluated using four evaluation criteria: knowledge and skill, mental demands, accountability, and working conditions. Points were assigned to each factor, and then the jobs that received the same points were judged to be of comparable worth to the state.

Although the decision did not go into detail about the jobs that were judged to be comparable, the following types of comparisons were made:

1. top level secretary ($1,400 per month) to electrician ($2,000)
2. laundry worker ($1,200) to truck driver ($1,650)
3. mental hospital counselor ($1,300) to heavy equipment operator ($1,800)
4. clerk typist ($1,050) to truck driver ($1,650).[57]

In each case, the first job represents the female-dominated classification and the latter the male. The pairs were judged by comparable-worth standards to be of equal worth.

According to Norman Willis, the 1974 comparable worth study revealed a tendency for women's classifications to be paid less for work judged to be comparable. This disparity averaged approximately 20%. The study also concluded that, as job values increased on the point scale, the disparity in pay tended to increase.

In December of 1974, Governor Evans held a press conference, at which time he acknowledged the results of the Willis study and said he thought "steps ought to be taken to rectify the imbalance which does exist."[58] An update of the initial study was conducted by Willis again in 1976, at which time 85 additional classifications were evaluated, and in December Governor Evans, just before leaving office, included a $7 million budget appropriation to start redressing the perceived inequities.

His successor, Governor Dixy Lee Ray removed that appropriation from the budget, even though the state had a surplus at the time. In 1980, she acknowledged in her Message to the Legislature that the survey revealed a 20% disparity and that the only thing the state had done about it was to conduct further updates of the original study (in all, four were conducted). She reported that the updates had revealed that the disparities were growing.

The state, after AFSCME filed the lawsuit, passed legislation to begin redressing the disparities, but the court judged the amount to be insufficient; a mere $1.5 million, which works out to $100.00 per employee per year, not to be payable until July 1984. Another bill called for implementation to be fully achieved by June 30, 1993.

AFSCME raised two novel theories of liability under Title VII, novel in the sense that they had not been applied successfully or even raised very often in comparable worth cases. These theories are "disparate impact" and "disparate treatment."

Disparate impact means that Title VII, as the courts have interpreted it , prohibits employment practices that, while facially neutral in practice, have a discriminatory impact on protected groups (race, color, religion, national origin, and sex) and are not justified by business necessity. Typically, this type of analysis is not applied to compensation claims, but to situations in which employment criteria, although seemingly neutral, affect protected groups in adverse ways: for example, height and weight requirements that disproportionately exclude women,[59] a requirement of a high school diploma or satisfactory performance on a standardized test that disproportionately affects minorities,[60] or a maternity leave policy that mandates immediate leave upon learning of pregnancy.[61] To prove disparate impact, no showing of an intent to discriminate has to be proven, the courts have held.[62] Disparate treatment means that, under Title VII, employment practices that intentionally and unfavorably treat employees based on impermissible criteria (race, color, sex, religion, national origin) are prohibited.[63] Disparate treatment can be proven by a plaintiff by the use of direct, circumstantial, and statistical evidence of discrimination.[64]

Judge Tanner, spurred by the Supreme Court's admonition in *Gunther* that, "Title VII's prohibition of discriminatory employment practices was intended to be broadly inclusive, proscribing 'not only overt discrimination but also practices that are fair in form, but discriminatory in operation,' "[65] found both disparate impact and disparate treatment analysis appropriate in this case.

He found for *AFSCME* on both of these theories of liability for employment discrimination. In respect to disparate impact, he concluded that the wage system in the State of Washington did have a disparate impact on female job classifications. Based on the state's own comparable worth studies, the state did not pay females in such classifications the full evaluated worth of their jobs. The state, he said, failed to produce credible evidence of an overriding business justification that would nullify the plaintiffs' evidence. Likewise, he found that the perpetuation of the wage system resulted in "intentional, unfavorable treatment of employees in predominately female job classifications," thus disparate treatment was proven.

This intent to discriminate he discerned in, among other things, the deliberate perpetuation of a 20% wage disparity, the admission of state officials that wages paid to women are discriminatory, and the state's failure to pay the plaintiffs their evaluated worth as established by the state's comparable worth study.[66]

In conclusion, Judge Tanner stated that he found this case "remarkably analogous to the recently decided *County of Washington v. Gunther* case."[67] While the case appeared to be novel, it wasn't really so, he argued, but was merely a failure-to-pay case. After all, he was not being asked to make judgments of comparable worth (something the courts have repeatedly expressed fear of being drawn into), but only to assume the conclusions of a comparable worth study already conducted by the state. Judge Tanner's remedies were extensive and costly; he granted a declaratory judgment against the state that it was in violation of Title VII and ordered injunctive relief and back pay beginning from September 16, 1979. He found bad faith on the part of the state, which justified in his mind the award of back pay.

Had the judgment of the district court been upheld, estimates of the cost of bringing the pay of female employees up to the levels required by the comparable worth study run between $400 and $848 million. But once offenses against Title VII have been initially proven (that is, a prima facie case has been established) the courts have consistently ruled that cost is no defense.

Judge Tanner turned a deaf ear to the state's argument that it is ironic that the State of Washington, which was the first in the country to consider the comparable worth rating system, should be penalized with such a devastating court ruling. He wrote:

> This court is of the opinion that it is indeed ironic and tragic that the State of Washington is in the eighth decade of the Twentieth Century attempting to use the American legal system to sanction, uphold and perpetuate sex bias. Defendants are struggling to maintain attitudes and concepts that are no longer acceptable under the provisions of Title VII.[68]

The irony, however, struck the Ninth Circuit Court of Appeals quite differently. They rejected AFSCME's argument that, once having commissioned a comparable worth study, the state is compelled to implement its findings. While they assumed that such a job evaluation study might be a useful tool, they rejected "a rule that would penalize rather than commend employers for their effort and innovation in undertaking such a study."[69]

They pointed to the variability in comparable worth studies and concluded from this that the result of any study should not "categorically bind" the employer who commissioned it. Rather, the employer should be free to take into account such considerations as market conditions, bargaining, demand, and the "possibility that another study will yield different results."[70]

Indeed, Judge (now Justice) Anthony Kennedy, writing for a unanimous three-judge panel, reversed the district court decision on both theories of liability under Title VII: disparate impact and disparate treatment. They found that disparate impact was not proven by the state's reliance in setting compensation on the market rather than the comparable worth studies. Nor could they discern discriminatory intent in the state's participation in the market, because the state did not create whatever disparity might exist in the marketplace, thus they concluded that the plaintiffs had failed to prove disparate treatment, as well. The appeals court seemed to embrace a much less liberal interpretation of *Gunther* than did Judge Tanner. While they acknowledged that *Gunther* broadened liability under Title VII beyond the "equal work" standard, they noted that the Supreme Court declined to define "the precise contours" of lawsuits challenging sex discrimination under Title VII, and that the court stated that *Gunther* did not involve the concept of comparable worth.

Judge Kennedy found that disparate impact analysis was erroneously employed by the lower court and ought to be confined to cases that challenge a specific, clearly delineated employment practice that is applied at a single point in the job selection process. Thus, the court held to the traditional view of disparate impact theory: that it is applicable only to cases where applicants are discriminated against by a policy (like height and weight regulations) that disproportionately weeds out women. Compensation decisions rely on too many factors to permit them to conform to the requirement of specificity necessary for disparate impact treatment.

Faulty, too, was Judge Tanner's finding for AFSCME on disparate treatment grounds. The appeals court concluded that the plaintiffs had failed to prove the requisite element of intent to discriminate. They rejected AFSCME's inference of intent from the Willis study and the state's reliance on the market to set wages—the market that, to AFSCME, embodied an historical pattern of discrimination against women. The court wrote:

> The requirement of intent is linked at least in part to culpability. . . . That concept would be undermined if we were to hold that payment of wages according to prevailing rates in the public and private sectors is an act that, in itself, supports the inference of a purpose to discriminate. Neither law nor logic deems the free market system a suspect enterprise. Economic reality is that the value of a particular job to an employer is but one factor influencing the rate of compensation for that job. Other considerations may include the availability of workers willing to do the job and the effectiveness of collective bargaining in a particular industry. . . . We find nothing in the language of Title VII or its legislative history to indicate Congress intended to abrogate fundamental economic principles such as the laws of supply and demand or to prevent employers from competing in the labor market.[71]

The court opined that, while Title VII did not obligate employers to eliminate an economic inequality they did not create, nothing prevents the legislature of the State of Washington from enacting a comparable worth system if it chooses.

The Ninth Circuit's decision should not have come as much of a surprise, considering that the same circuit rejected a comparable worth theory in a case decided a year earlier.[72] Nevertheless, the decision generated a maelstrom of outrage, from AFSCME, women's groups, and, of course, some of the beneficiaries of the earlier decision in the ranks of Washington's female employees. Curiously, later that year, on New Year's Eve to be exact, the State of Washington reached an agreement with AFSCME and the other union that had brought suit. The settlement granted nearly $500 million to women workers in order to achieve pay equity by 1992, and it came only hours before a January 1 deadline set by the legislature for disposing of the comparable worth controversy. (The law mandating implementation of comparable worth that the state had enacted in 1983 was still in force, nothing in the appeals court decision having negated it).[73] Thus, the case never reached the Supreme Court.

AFSCME continues to remain active in the comparable worth cause, pursuing court cases, testifying before congressional committees, promoting the cause in the states, and raising the issues in collective bargaining. Over the years, this union has been among the most active promoters of comparable worth. AFSCME local 101 led the San Jose city workers in their strike over pay equity in July of 1981. The strike ended after nine days, when the city agreed to a $1.5 pay equity kitty.

AFSCME has also pursued pay equity in Los Angeles, both through collective bargaining and EEOC charges. It is pursuing similar efforts in other municipalities and states. Its efforts in the courts have been manifold, including lawsuits against Connecticut and Nassau County, New York; and it has filed numerous EEOC charges against states, cities, school districts, and other agencies.[74] AFSCME zealousness in pursuit of comparable worth claims is not surprising, considering its high proportion of female members.

One other post-*Gunther* decision deserves mention, for it too declined to broaden Title VII to include pure comparable worth claims. This case, *American Nurses Association v. State of Illinois* (1986),[75] was decided by a unanimous three judge panel of the Seventh Circuit, and the decision was written by Judge Richard Posner, a Reagan appointee and prominent figure among the law and economics school. He was joined in the decision by Judge Frank Easterbrook, another Reagan appointee, and like Posner, a former faculty member of the law school at the University of Chicago.

The case was brought by nurses and typists under Title VII and the Fourteenth Amendment's equal protection clause. They complained that the state pays workers in predominantly male job classifications more than it pays women in female-dominated jobs, and that this disparity is not justified by any differences in the relative worth of the jobs. Furthermore, they charged that the state failed to implement the results of a comparable worth study.

While the court was dealing with a technical issue—whether the district court acted properly in dismissing the suit on the ground that a comparable worth plea failed to state a violation of antidiscrimination law—the decision did include some interesting ruminations on comparable worth. Posner wrote:

> . . . economists point out that the ratio of wages in different jobs is determined by the market rather than by any a priori conception of relative merit, in just the same way that the ratio of the price of caviar to the price of cabbage is determined by relative scarcity rather than relative importance to human welfare.[76]

The decision was not noticeably sympathetic to comparable worth, with the court stating that the "issue of comparable worth . . . is not of the sort that judges are well equipped to resolve intelligently or that we should lightly assume has been given to us to resolve by Title VII or the Constitution.''[77]

Even though the court reversed and remanded the case, on the ground that the plaintiffs deserved the chance to prove the elements of their case that alleged intentional discrimination, the judges warned that the nurses would have a ''tough row to hoe.''[78] What is clear from this rather complex decision is that, if the plaintiffs had merely complained about the state's failure to implement a comparable worth study, they would have had no case.[79]

Final Reflections

Comparable worth suits of the *AFSCME* sort continue to crop up in the courts. The Pennsylvania Nurses Association, for example, has filed suit, charging the Commonwealth of Pennsylvania with violating Title VII by paying and classifying women in a discriminatory fashion. The suit is based on a study showing that 80% of the job classifications are either female or male dominated, and that women are clustered in the lowest-paying rungs.[80] Despite ultimate defeat in *AFSCME v. Washington*—at least defeat in the courts, for one could hardly call a $500 million settlement a defeat— comparable worth's supporters have not given up.

From the previous discussion, it is apparent that the courts have not been enthusiastic about comparable worth; quite the contrary. Courts have been reluctant to get involved in making independent judgments about the comparability of disparate jobs; and they have only been slightly less chary about intervening to mandate implementation where states have conducted such studies. Indeed, only Judge Tanner in *AFSCME* has dared to take the latter plunge. But the courts have given enough hope—particularly the Supreme Court's nebulous decision in *Gunther*—to keep the cases coming.

One wonders whether congressional intent is as murky as the Supreme Court in *Gunther* made out. What is unambiguous is that in 1963, when Congress enacted the Equal Pay Act, it explicitly rejected comparisons of dissimilar jobs and replaced that wide notion with ''equal work.'' Those who spoke in support of such a change clearly intended that the substitution would narrow the purview of the act to those instances in which women were doing the same work as men but were, nevertheless, paid less. What they wanted to avoid was federal bureaucrats going into places of employment and imposing their arbitrary and fluctuating standards of comparison. As Representative Goodell, cosponsor of the act, remarked on the change from ''comparable'' to ''equal'':

> I think it is important that we have clear legislative history at this point. Last year, when the House changed the word 'comparable' to 'equal', the clear intention was to narrow the whole concept. We went from 'comparable' to 'equal'

> meaning that the jobs involved should be virtually identical, that is, that they would be very much alike or closely related to each other.
>
> We do not expect the Labor Department to go into an establishment and attempt to rate jobs that are not equal. We do not want to hear the department say, "Well, they amount to the same thing," and evaluate them so that they come up to the same skill or point. We expect this to apply only to jobs that are substantially identical or equal.[81]

The legislative intent on the Equal Pay Act is unambiguous, as all parties to the dispute agree.

But what about Title VII? It stretches credulity beyond the breaking point to presume that Congress intended something different for wage disparities due to sex in 1964 than it did in 1963. Why? For the simple reasons that no hearings were held on the issue, the category of sex was introduced by Southern elements who opposed the whole bill and would vote against it in the end, and nothing said at the time indicates that any broadening was intended. In fact, whatever slim evidence there is of contemporaneous intent leans heavily the other way. The Bennett Amendment, if it is not simply superfluous, must mean something in addition to the affirmative defenses that were already in Title VII before the amendment was introduced. The only element that the Bennett Amendment could have added from the Equal Pay Act that was not already included was the "equal work" standard.

Senator Clark, the floor manager for the bill, replied to an objection by Senator Dirksen that the title extended far beyond the scope of the Equal Pay Act because it did not include the "equal work" standard, in the following words:

> . . . The standards in the Equal Pay Act for determining discrimination as to wages, of course, are applicable to the comparable situation under title VII.[82]

But Senator Bennett wanted to add more insurance that this interpretation would hold up in the courts, so he added his amendment. He stated his purpose thusly:

> The purpose of my amendment is to provide that in the event of conflicts, the provisions of the Equal Pay Act shall not be nullified.[83]

Senator Bennett, one year later, provided a written understanding of the amendment in which he stated that, "the amendment means that discrimination in compensation on account of sex does not violate Title VII unless it also violates the Equal Pay Act."[84]

The majority of the Supreme Court chose to finesse the Bennett Amendment as a mere technical correction. While Senator Bennett himself referred to it as such, the court seemed to give too narrow an interpretation to the term 'technical correction.' It is clear from his contemporaneous statement what he meant.

The court found the 'equal work' standard too confining, so it chose to play rather loosely with the record. Indeed, a comparison of two of the court's statements will make this clear:

> . . . although the few references by Members of Congress to the Bennett Amendment do not explicitly confirm that its purpose was to incorporate into Title VII the four affirmative defenses of the Equal Pay Act in sex-based wage discrimination cases, they are broadly consistent with such a reading, and do not support an alternative reading.[85]

> . . . Title VII's prohibition of discriminatory employment practices was intended to be broadly inclusive, proscribing 'not only overt discrimination but also practices that are fair in form, but discriminatory in operation.'[86]

The first statement bespeaks a certain hesitancy, while the second imputes sweeping intentions to Congress. One tends to sympathize with the court's dissenters on this one, when they charged that the court had certain policy objectives it wished to achieve, and if Title VII replete with the Bennett Amendment was too narrow to accomplish these objectives, then it would have to be widened.

With the Supreme Court declining to enter the fray since *Gunther*, the lower courts are left to their own devices, and the judicial landscape will remain diverse, complex, and somewhat befuddling. With such confusion, comparable worth's advocates have just enough encouragement to keep them litigating. What would put an end to such litigation, or at least most of it, would be a clear Supreme Court decision reading Title VII as incorporating the Equal Pay Act's "equal work" standard. That seems unlikely, given the court's reluctance to overrule itself, but, on the other hand, it seems entirely justifiable. The court is more likely to keep ducking the issue until more comparable worth cases are won at the appeals court level (and more lost), and a decision seems unavoidable.

Comparable Worth in the Federal Government and the States

Comparable worth has not been enacted by Congress, but this has not been for lack of trying. A comparable worth bill (H.R. 5680), the first ever to have reached the floor of the House, passed overwhelmingly in July of 1984 with a 413-to-6 majority. The bill, the "Pay Equity and Management Act of 1984," called for a study of pay differentials in the federal government between female job classifications and "comparable" male classifications. What eventually passed the Senate was a bill on Civil Service Amendments, but one denuded of its call for a comparable worth study. In a compromise between the two houses, a GAO study was called for that would examine the most desirable methodology for federal pay classifications, but no legislation was implemented based on that study. Spurred by the lopsided victory in the House, the comparable worth forces held hearings on an even more ambitious measure (H.R. 5092) that would have extended the concept of comparable worth as a wage-setting standard to the private sector.

In 1985, the House again passed legislation calling for a study of the federal bureaucracy (H.R. 3008), but this time the vote was much closer, dividing along party lines. The Senate Committee on Governmental Affairs declined to hold hearings on the bill, and thus it died in committee. Measures of a similar type have been introduced in subsequent sessions of Congress, but it remains to be seen how the bills will fare in a Congress now dominated in both its chambers by Democrats. Even if a bill were to pass both houses, it would likely face a presidential veto, as the Reagan administration, in marked contrast to its predecessor, has been noticeably inhospitable to the comparable worth concept.

Comparable Worth in the Federal Agencies

During the Carter years, comparable worth enjoyed much support among administrative agencies. For example, Eleanor Holmes Norton as head of the Equal Employment Opportunity Commission (EEOC), selected the comparable worth issue as one of the priorities of her tenure. Indeed, upon leaving office in 1981, she was influential in the formation of the National Committee on Pay Equity. While still chairing the EEOC, she commissioned a study of the comparable worth issue by the prestigious National Research Council (NRC) of the National Academy of Sciences.

The Committee on Occupational Classification and Analysis, which was formed by the NRC to study the question, issued a report in August of 1981, *Women, Work, and Wages*, edited by Donald J. Treiman and Heidi I. Hartmann. That study, while not an unqualified endorsement of the comparable worth concept, nevertheless concluded that the existing labor markets were tainted by discrimination.

> A major portion of our early discussion focused on whether, in fact, the existing wage rate is a good approximation of the worth of a job. Our ultimate view . . . is that the substantial influence of institutional and traditional arrangements makes it impossible to view current wage rates as set solely by the free play of neutral forces operating in an entirely open market, no matter how attractive such a theoretical formulation may be.[87]

The majority report questioned, however, whether the means for effecting a comparable worth remedy were refined enough, that is, whether job evaluation schemes could be applied throughout the economy when value or worth cannot be determined by scientific methods.[88] Thus, they confined their study to the implementation of comparable worth within firms, arguing that the concept "merits consideration. . .wherever women are systematically underpaid."[89]

The Office of Federal Contract Compliance Programs (OFCCP) under the Carter administration also was an enthusiastic advocate of comparable worth. The OFCCP is the agency charged with administering compliance to affirmative action under Executive Order 11246, the order that mandated federal contractors to engage in "affirmative action" on behalf of women and minorities. Comparable worth language was inserted in the agency's sex discrimination guidelines, although the revisions were not scheduled to take effect until the Carter days had ended. The language was subsequently jettisoned by the Reagan administration.[90]

As Reagan succeeded Carter, hostility toward comparable worth replaced sympathy. On June 18, 1985 the EEOC, under the direction of its chairman, Clarence Thomas, issued a unanimous ruling that rejected the extension of Title VII of the Civil Rights Act of 1964 to include comparable worth comparisons. The case was brought to the EEOC—the agency responsible for enforcing both the Equal Pay Act and Title VII—by women employees of the Housing Authority of Rockford, Illinois. The women were represented by the American Federation of State, County, and Municipal Employees. They alleged that the housing authority paid employees in traditionally female-dominated job categories less than employees in traditionally male-dominated jobs, even though the duties the women performed required "equal or more skill, effort, and responsibility than the duties performed by employees in classifications traditionally and predominately occupied by male employees."[91]

The housing authority's staff is divided into two groups: one, administrative staff, is 85% female; the other, maintenance staff, is 88% male. The women did not allege, nor did the EEOC's investigators discern, that the employer assigned employees to jobs on the basis of sex nor that any barriers were erected to prevent the movement of the sexes between the two job categories. (Such a finding, of course, would have constituted an unmistakable breach of Title VII.) Having found no such direct or circumstantial evidence that the difference in pay between the men and women was due to sex, the commission concluded that it could not infer that sex was a factor in wage setting. The commission stated:

> Rather than being based on evidence of intentional discrimination, the Charging Parties' claim appears to be based on what the Supreme Court referred to as "the controversial concept of 'comparable worth.' " Gunther, 452 U.S. at 166.

Under this theory, individuals claim entitlement to "increased compensation on the basis of a comparison of the intrinsic worth or difficulty of their job with that of other jobs in the same organization or community." Id. The Commission finds no statutory basis or case law support for the conclusion that evidence consisting solely of such a comparison is sufficient to establish a violation of Title VII.[92]

After examining the case law, both before and after *Gunther*, and finding nothing to support a Title VII claim solely on comparable worth grounds, the commission concluded:

The Commission is convinced that Congress never consented to wholesale governmental restructuring of the valuations of jobs established by the nonsex-based decisions of employers, the collective bargaining process, or by the mechanisms of the market place.[93]

Predictably, the commission's decision met with mixed reviews. The U.S. Chamber of Commerce and the National Association of Manufacturers hailed the decision, with the NAM's executive vice president, Jerry Jasinowski, expressing a good deal of relief. "Employers should rest easier," he said, with the knowledge that the commission "will not get into the business of determining the inherent worth of jobs."

By contrast, Winn Newman, a lawyer who frequently argues comparable worth cases for AFSCME and other unions, denounced the decision, declaring that the commission was "perpetuating sex discrimination and playing into the hands of sex bigots."[94] It should be noted that all of the members of the commission are Reagan-era appointees. The contrast between the Carter and Reagan eras on comparable worth could not be starker than at the EEOC.

The U.S. Civil Rights Commission, under the direction of its colorful and controversial chairman, Clarence Pendleton, Jr., has also taken a stand against comparable worth. This commission, although it has no enforcement power, is supposed to serve as a moral conscience to the nation on civil rights issues. In the Reagan years, it has proven a hotbed of intrigue and the source of much chagrin on Capitol Hill and among the commission's traditional civil-rights constituency.

In 1983, the president generated a maelstrom with his attempt to replace the commissioners hospitable to affirmative action with new ones more to his liking. The 99th Congress and the commission were virtually at war, with threats flying to disband the commission, and finally resulting in a truncated budget for it in 1987. Several commissioners and high-level staff people resigned in disgust.

The Civil Rights Commission on April 11, 1985, declared in a 5-2 vote its opposition to the concept of comparable worth, calling it "unsound and misplaced.'' This decision was not reached in isolation or disregard for the wealth of argument on both sides of the debate, for, in June of 1984, the commission had conducted a two-day consultation on comparable worth that included the preparation of papers and testimony by many of the leading figures on both sides of the controversy. Linda Chavez, then serving as staff director of the commission, was instrumental in suggesting the consultation, although she herself was on record as opposing comparable worth. That consultation led to a two-volume publication, *Comparable Worth: Issues for the 80s*, which is probably the most quoted source in subsequent writings on the topic.

The commission's majority urged Congress and the federal enforcement agencies to reject the concept of comparable worth in setting wages in federal or private-sector jobs. Chairman Pendleton—who received much national attention with his quip that comparable worth was the looniest idea since Loony Tunes—said adoption of the concept would be ''a disingenuous attempt to restructure our free enterprise system into a state-controlled economy under the guise of 'fairness.' ''

The commission, in its statement on comparable worth, contended that pay disparities between men and women are caused often by factors other than discrimination, factors including unequal educational backgrounds and skills. It also criticized the job-evaluation systems that are used to implement the comparable-worth concept as being ''inherently subjective.''

Morris Abram, vice president of the commission, said comparable worth would amount to ''permanent government wage control over a substantial, if not the majority, of the working population, and I don't think this country is ready for it.''[95]

Carter-era commissioners, Mary Frances Berry and Blandina Cardenas Ramierez, dissented, contending that the concept of pay equity ''should be applied prudently with a full recognition of any limitations that might exist. . . . But its use can be an important tool in the arsenal for attacking employment discrimination.''[96]

The commission's decision was roundly denounced by the presidents of the National Committee on Pay Equity and AFSCME. Judy Goldsmith, then president of the National Organization for Women, described the commission's report as ''an abomination'' and ''anti-woman.''

Other organs of the federal bureaucracy in the Reagan years have also expressed their disapproval of, if not outright hostility to, the comparable worth concept. These include the Office of Personnel Management, whose former director, Donald Devine, had a run-in with Congress over this issue when he tried to forestall the passage of the 1984 comparable worth bill. The bill, despite his attempts at marshalling opposition to it, nevertheless passed the House overwhelmingly, but was amended by Representative Oakar to preclude the OPM from conducting the study that the legislation mandated. The Justice Department, particularly its assistant attorney general for civil rights,

William Bradford Reynolds, has also generated its share of turmoil over comparable worth. Reynolds announced, shortly after the district court's decision favorable to comparable worth in the *AFSCME* case, that the Justice Department might join the appeal in behalf of the State of Washington. Again, the comparable worth activists vehemently protested.

For comparable worth enthusiasts, the record of the Reagan years is certainly discouraging. Seemingly blocked at every turn—by hostile presidential appointees at the bureaucratic agencies and by a balky Senate dominated until early 1987 by Republicans—the pay equity champions have found little to cheer about at the federal level of government. In the states, however, matters have proceeded in quite a different direction, providing the supporters with some sweet victories.

The States: Comparable Worth Sweeps the Nation

While disappointments abound for comparable worth's supporters in the courts and at the federal level, such is not the case in the states. Since 1981, the states have been a hotbed of activity, with the less zealous ones adopting legislation calling for comparable worth studies and the more activist actually implementing pay rectification schemes based upon the results of such studies.[97] Minnesota, Idaho, New York, Iowa, Massachusetts, New Mexico, and Washington have begun the process of adjusting salaries of female state employees after conducting comparable worth evaluations. Numerous other states have passed legislation that either directed state agencies to conduct or commission comparable worth studies or declared, as in California in 1981, that it is state policy to compensate women in female-dominated state jobs on the basis of the "comparability of the value of the work."

The National Committee on Pay Equity estimated that, by the end of 1986, thirteen states would have begun the process of distributing pay–equity adjustments while thirty-four other states would be moving in the same direction. These figures may be somewhat optimistic. In September 1986, the General Accounting Office prepared a report to Senators Alan Cranston and Daniel Evans based on a questionnaire and interviews conducted with personnel officers in each of the states. The report concluded that ten of the states had a written pay equity or comparable worth policy, while twenty-eight states in all had conducted some type of comparable worth study.[98]

Labor unions have been instrumental in some states in either conducting comparable worth studies of their own or in lobbying for the enactment of comparable worth legislation. In Pennsylvania, for example, Council 13 of AFSCME had its Comparable Worth Committee commission two industrial psychologists at Temple University to conduct a study of the state job-classification system. They concluded, after examining a select group of job titles, that the average differential between male- and female-dominated jobs was $1.10 per hour.[99] Similar disparities were discerned in Ohio, where a Pay Equity subcommittee of the House found that women received 87 cents per hour less then men. The committee recommended that this pay gap be eliminated and that the state adopt comparable worth as the primary factor in establishing salaries, both for public and private jobs.[100]

Minnesota has been at the forefront of comparable worth activity, and it is one of the handful of states that has actually appropriated funds to rectify perceived inequities. Minnesota's efforts began in 1979, with a study conducted by Hay Associates for the Department of Employee Relations. The Hay study employed a point/factor methodology, with points assigned to jobs based on four factors: know-how, problem solving, accountability, and working conditions. The value of each job was then determined by adding up the points attained for each factor.

A legislative advisory council conducted another Hay study in 1981, which discovered salary disparities between male- and female-dominated job classifications. On average, the pay of women was found to be 25% lower than men's salaries. The average female employee with twenty years of experience was found to make less than the average newly hired male state employee.[101] The advisory council recommended that money be appropriated to eliminate the inequity, estimating that the yearly cost for implementation would be $26 million. A pay equity policy was established by state law in 1982. For the biennium beginning in January of 1983, the legislature appropriated $21.8 million for pay equity raises. The plan anticipated a four-year implementation schedule that would achieve full parity. Approximately 8,225 employees received pay equity adjustments, with clerical workers receiving $1,601 on average and health care workers slightly higher over the two-year period. The Minnesota legislature, in 1984, extended pay equity to cities, counties, and school districts.[102] This extension of comparable worth to local governments is particularly ambitious, covering 163,000 workers in 1,400 political subdivisions.

Because the Minnesota plan did not cut the salaries of male employees, it was uncontroversial in its early stages. However, controversy was not too long in coming. By 1985, the police and firefighters' unions began to lobby in the legislature to be excluded from the comparable worth scheme.

"The firefighters went crazy," an official of the Minnesota Association of Commerce and Industry remarked, "because the point system classifies a librarian's job the same level as a fireman's job. One fireman testified that he knows a librarian's job is very dangerous—'a book could fall on her head.' "[103] Republicans in the legislature and the U.S. Chamber of Commerce have begun seriously worrying about the cost and complexity of implementing comparable worth in Minnesota's localities.

Comparable worth has achieved some successes, too, at the local level, with the Los Angeles City Council, for one, agreeing to approve pay increases of 15% for 3,900 employees, most of whom are female clerks and librarians. The city acquiesced to these increases in order to settle a sex discrimination complaint. Over a three-year period, the city plans to spend $36 million raising the wages of its female workers. Several other cities have begun to gather information and conduct studies, including Fresno, San Francisco, and Berkeley in California, and pay equity increases have been negotiated by AFSCME in San Mateo, California, Green Bay, Wisconsin, and Belmont, California.

These victories have not come easily. In San Jose, AFSCME, Local 101 pressured the city for a comparable worth study, and after some resistance by the city manager and the council a study was conducted by Hay Associates. Not surprisingly, the study discovered a wage disparity adversely affecting women, with female-dominated jobs receiving from 2% to 10% less than the rate for all jobs in the city. A complaint was filed with the EEOC after negotiations failed to remedy the situation, and the city manager broke off negotiations. In July of 1981, AFSCME conducted an illegal strike, which after one week resulted in an agreement that, while not an overt endorsement of the comparable worth concept, nevertheless did secure salary increased for female workers.[104]

Comparable Worth Abroad

Concern about achieving equal pay for women is not unique to the United States. In fact, two countries are usually cited by supporters as having moved far in advance of the United States toward embracing a comparable worth standard: Canada and Australia. Beyond these, however, equal pay for equal work or equal pay for work of equal value has been enshrined in several multinational agreements. The International Labor Organization (ILO), a specialized agency of the United Nations, drafted Convention No. 100, entitled Equal Remuneration between Men and Women, in 1951. This convention, signed now by 80 countries, declares that signatory nations shall "ensure the application to all workers of the principle of equal remuneration for men and women workers *for work of equal value*" (emphasis added). However, the convention does not define what is meant by "work of equal value," nor does it give any guidance about how "equal value" is to be determined. One authority, who has studied the genesis of this convention, concluded that nothing more was intended by this language than an endorsement of the "equal pay for equal work" concept and that a comparable worth interpretation of the language would be misleading.[105]

Another multinational document has equal pay connotations, although here its subsequent history seemingly has gone beyond its original intent. The Treaty of Rome, which established the European Economic Community (EEC) in 1957, contains an Article 119 that states in its English translation: "Each Member State shall during the first stage ensure and subsequently maintain the application of the principle that men and women should receive *equal pay for equal work*."

In the early years, the document was interpreted as guaranteeing something less encompassing than the ILO's "equal value" standard, but in 1975, an equal-pay directive was adopted that went beyond the language of Article 119. This directive states that the principle of equal pay contained in Article 119 of the Treaty of Rome has the following meaning: equal pay "for the same work or for work to which equal value is attributed. . . . In particular, where a job classification system is used for determining pay, it must be based on the same criteria for both men and women and so drawn up as to exclude any discrimination on grounds of sex."

Equal value, once again, is left undefined. Member states were required to pass suitable legislation and enforcement mechanisms, and, by 1979, a report was issued that was very critical of the inadequacy of the efforts in seven countries. The report indicated that "equal value" should be given a broad interpretation, for a narrow one would negate the equal-pay guarantee. The history of the interpretation of this document, then, seems clearly to be moving in a comparable worth direction.[106]

Canada has taken strides toward embracing a comparable worth interpretation of equal pay, but the extent of its movement in that direction is a subject of some controversy. At least the early cases decided under its Human Rights Act of 1977 do not appear to go beyond what could be easily contained within our own Equal Pay Act of 1963 (which mandates only an "equal work" standard). But it is clear from the writings of one of its leading interpreters, Rita Cadieux, the Deputy Chief Commissioner of the Canadian Human Rights Commission since its inception in 1977, that the Human Rights Act will be used as an engine for achieving comparable worth.[107]

Section 11 of the Canadian Human Rights Act embraces the "equal value" standard:

(1) It is a discriminatory practice for an employer to establish or maintain differences in wages between male and female employees employed in the same establishment who are performing work of equal value.
(2) In assessing the value of work performed by employees employed in the same establishment the criterion to be applied is the composite of the skill, effort, and responsibility required in the performance of the work and the conditions under which the work is performed.

The Human Rights Act is limited in its purview, extending only to about

11% of Canada's workers, those working in the federal public service, Crown corporations, and employees of federally regulated companies such as those in transportation, communication, and banking. The limited extent of the act is a result of Canada's division of responsibility for regulating labor relations between the central government and the provinces. Most employees, then, fall under provincial regulation. But the Human Rights Act certainly serves as an example to the provinces. Canada, like the United States, has a wage disparity between full-time working women and men, with the women earning about 62% of the average salary of men.

The commission promulgated guidelines interpreting Section 11 in 1978; these guidelines, in addition to defining the key terms in the provisions cited above, also laid out some factors that would legitimate differences in wages between men and women. These factors include: different performance ratios, seniority, red circling (where a position is reevaluated and downgraded), a temporary rehabilitation assignment, a demotion, phased-in wage reductions, a temporary training position. The guidelines were amended in 1982 to allow for changes in wages due to a labor shortage or to permit situations in which the value of a job is decreased without the salary being lowered.

The commission proceeds by investigating complaints brought by individuals, groups of workers, the commission itself, or, more often, unions. A comparison group is identified, then the commission sends compensation experts out to the work place to audit the jobs. They assess the jobs using the skill, effort, responsibility, and conditions of work criteria embodied in the guidelines.

A factor/point analysis is performed to establish the value of the jobs. "What is different, under the act," writes the commission's deputy director, "is that internal equity is established without reference to the marketplace. The so-called market value is often distorted by society's perception of women's work as having limited value."[108] If an inequity is found to exist, the commission tries to settle the dispute, and, if this fails, the commission may call a human rights tribunal, which has the power to order a balky employer to rectify the situation. These orders can be appealed in the federal court.

Early cases tended to mimic ours under the Equal Pay Act, with female nurses, for example, charging that male "health care officers," who performed work of equal value, received more pay. Here, the commission's assessment was that the work was the same, and they reached a settlement with the government employer that resulted in average wage increases of $1000 for the nurses, plus $18,000 in retroactive pay.

More recent settlements have departed from the "equal work" model, encompassing comparisons of jobs that are not the same. Librarians charged that they were under-compensated in comparison to Historical Research workers, and the commission found in the librarians' favor after performing a regression analysis to compare the jobs in the two specialties. Librarians received a total settlement of $2.3 million from their employer, the Federal Treasury Board, which included a portion for retroactive compensation. Another case—one involving food, laundry, and other service groups—brought against the Treasury Board resulted in an even larger settlement: a total of $17 million.[109] The commission, at least as of 1984, had not gotten involved in the broader comparable-worth-type comparisons—for example, of nurse and tree-trimmers, or secretaries and truck drivers.

The equal pay situation is much different in Australia, which since the turn of the century has set wages for almost all occupations by federal and state wage tribunals. Thus, Australia does not have a free labor marketplace; rather, wages are set by boards that operate under egalitarian-promoting principles that look to narrow the wage gap between various occupations and to secure the same wage rates for a particular occupation across industries. And, until 1969, wages were explicitly set on a two-tier basis, with women's wages generally fixed at 54% of men's wages before World War II and at 75% after 1950.

During the war years, women who filled the jobs previously held by males who had gone off to war were compensated at 90% of the male rate. The tribunals set minimum wages for each occupation, with employers and employees left free to negotiate over-awards in a modified collective bargaining process. Male wages were fixed by the tribunals to support a man along with his wife and children "living in a civilized community"; female wages were set to support a single woman. Various grades of labor were apportioned additional compensation based on their "work value," thus the award for each type of labor would comprise the minimum for a decent standard of living plus something extra for the skill necessary to accomplish the job. The latter criterion was, also, not applied neutrally as between the sexes.

In 1969 this sex-segregated system began to change. The federal tribunal— the Commonwealth Conciliation and Arbitration Commission—handed down a decision that accepted the principle of equal pay for work of "the same or a like nature and of equal value." This meant women who performed the same work as men would receive the same pay, but this decision only covered about 20% of the female work force.

A 1972 decision went even further by establishing "equal pay for work of equal value" to be phased in by 1975. This decision ended the two-tier wage system in Australia by covering women in sex-segregated occupations, in addition to those already covered by the 1969 decision. This was an important step, because Australia's labor market was and remains highly segmented by sex.

By 1977, the wage gap between men and women in the same job classifications had declined from 25% in 1969 to 7%, with the remaining differential resulting from union negotiated over-awards. Earnings of full-time working women on average were 75.3% of male earnings, while awards for females were 93.1% of those for males as of 1981. This represents a dramatic improvement over the two figures for 1969, which were 58.4% and 72% respectively.[110]

Is the Australian model really relevant to the debate over comparable worth in the United States? In one sense, it is clearly not, since as compared with Australia we have a relatively free labor market. True, we have our minimum wage law and our National Labor Relations Act, which constrain the market in various ways, but we do not have wage tribunals setting the rates of pay for all or any occupations in the country.

In another sense, however, the Australian model is pertinent to the debate. I will contend in the next chapter that one implication of instituting comparable worth in the United States would be the necessity of having boards set the salaries of all occupations. Perhaps we would not establish entities called wage boards—as our Australian friends have with their Commonwealth Conciliation and Arbitration Council and their special Commonwealth Industrial Courts. We might leave it up to our federal courts to serve in their stead; but the implications would be the same: We would no longer be free to bargain for our wages. Regardless of whether my argument will be convincing, one lesson of the Australian experience should be apparent, and that is that what the wage board giveth the wage board may taketh away. Any board that has the power to discriminate against women—as the Australian board did for 71 years (from 1904-1975)—and decides to end such discrimination still has the power to discriminate: against or in favor of which groups in the future, one can only speculate.

Conclusion

Comparable worth's supporters have enjoyed their share of victories, mostly achieved at the state level. Many states began to consider comparable worth for their state employees after the district court decision in *AFSCME v. Washington*. Studies were conducted, comparable worth pay adjustments were distributed, and legislation enacted, sometimes out of fear of lawsuits and always with the support of feminist groups. While the decision favorable to comparable worth in that case was overturned, it took several years before that happened, and, in the intervening time, comparable worth gained considerable momentum.

The forces of pay equity cannot but be disappointed by the reversal in this case, a case that captured public attention for their cause. For despite the seeming room left open for comparable worth challenges by the Supreme Court's decision in *Gunther v. Washington*, other courts have not been very receptive to cases brought under a comparable worth interpretation of Title VII. In fact, *Gunther* has not really changed the courts' attitudes much on this score. Disappointing, also, has been the reversal of the support for comparable worth in the federal agencies under the Carter administration by the Reagan team. Sympathy has been replaced by outright hostility.

Yet these reversals have not dimmed the enthusiasm of comparable worth's proponents. Indeed, they have seemed to pursue their goal with added determination and vigor. Court cases and bills before Congress proliferate in exponential fashion. Every defeat seems to inspire renewed efforts and heighten the passion of the pay equity enthusiasts.

Notes

1. *American Federation of State, County, and Municipal Employees v. State of Washington*, 578 F. Supp. 846 (1983).
2. The sense of 'compared' meant here is not the same as 'comparable' worth; rather it captures the sense of jobs that are substantially equivalent, the sense intended by the Equal Pay Act.
3. The Equal Pay Act of 1963, 29 U.S.C.206(d); Title VII of the Civil Rights Act of 1964, 42 U.S.C. §200e, 78 Stat. 253.
4. It should be noted that "comparable work" and "comparable worth" are not synonymous terms, although they are often used loosely and interchangeably. The first is narrower, implying merely that the jobs are closely enough allied to be compared; but it is a looser standard than "equal work." "Comparable worth" implies that the jobs are worth the same to the employer, even though they might be as different as tree trimmer and secretary.
5. See: *Laffey v. Northwest Airlines, Inc.*, 35 FEP Cases 508 (CA DC, 1984), in which the U.S. Court of Appeals for the District of Columbia held that the airlines violated the Equal Pay Act for paying male "pursers" more than female "stewardesses" for doing the same work.
6. It should be mentioned, also, that the Equal Pay Act has been amended in 1966, 1972, and 1974 to widen its sweep by enlarging the definition of "employer" to include state and local workers in hospitals, institutions, schools, and public agencies. Covered too are executives, professionals, and administrators.
7. The courts have labored to define the various elements of this definition, beginning with equal work. *Equal work*—here, the courts have generated a concept of "substantially the same" or "substantially equal" work, which does not mean identical work, but rather work that is alike enough that minor variations in the frequency of certain duties are judged insignificant.

    Equal skill—the assessment of equal skill depends on the experience, training, education, and ability required in the performance of the two jobs being compared. The judgment does not depend upon the efficiency of the employee nor upon any additional training that one set of employees might possess, but on the nature of the duties as performed (so that additional skills, if not germane to the job, will be ignored in the assessment). See: *Peltier v. City of Fargo*, 12 FEP Cases 945 (CA 8, 1976); *Brennan v. Owensboro-Daviess County Hospital*, 11 FEP Cases 600 (Ca 6, 1975), in which the court concluded that wage differentials between female nursing aides and male orderlies was unjustified by the standards of the Equal Pay Act, despite the fact that orderlies performed additional duties, such as removing casts and carrying oxygen tanks. The court stated that these extra tasks consumed a negligible amount of the orderlies' workday.

Equal Effort—An often cited case on the equal effort standard (*Hodgson v. Brookhaven General Hospital*, 9 FEP Cases 579 (CA 5, 1972) sets out this test: Equal effort is not demonstrated if the more highly paid job involves additional tasks that require extra effort, consume a significant amount of the time of all those whose pay differentials are to be justified, and are of an economic value commensurate with the pay differential. *Equal Responsibility*—The degree of responsibility is at issue here, thus, extra pay for one who assumes supervisory functions is justifiable. *Similar Working Conditions*—Differences in working conditions as between inside and outside work can be significant. While courts have said that differentials in pay between day and night shifts are sometimes permissible, the Supreme Court in *Corning Glass Works v. Brennan*, 417 U.S. 188 (1974) found that such a differential violated the Equal Pay Act. The court found that "working conditions" has a specific meaning in industrial relations that includes "surroundings" and "hazards" but not shifts. But the court did allow some room for nondiscriminatory pay differentials under the act in the fourth exception, that "based on any other factor other than sex."

In Corning's case, however, the court did not discern such a nondiscriminatory purpose (one that would compensate the men on the night shift for psychological or physiological detriments of night work), but rather viewed the payments as simply extra pay based upon sex. (at 204-205)

8. This fourth exception (or defense) is broad. Courts have held: that it is permissible to raise the salaries of female faculty members pursuant to an affirmative action plan and a federal government finding that the university had discriminated against women faculty (*Ende v. Board of Regents of Regency University*, 37 FEP Cases 575 (CA7, 1985); that it is permissible for an employer to revise its job evaluation and pay scale, provided that the reorganization is not a subterfuge for paying women less (*Patkus v. Sangamon-Cass Consortium*, 38 FEP Cases 1272 (CA7, 1985); state regulations that distinguish between jobs, when the distinction seems valid to the court can also qualify as a "factor other than sex"; in *Hodgson v. Robert Hall Clothes, Inc.*, 11 FEP Cases 1271 (CA3, 1973) the court upheld pay differences between salespersons of men's and women's clothing based on the greater profitability of the men's clothing department.

Other factors that courts have considered include: business reasons may justify setting entry level salaries based on prior salaries, even if women's salaries have been historically lower (the court would have to assess whether such lower payments are pretexts for discrimination); awarding salary increases to match outside offers. For a fuller discussion of these cases, see: "Equal Pay Act," *Fair Employment Practices*, The Bureau of National Affairs, at 421:308-421:312.

9. *Corning Glass Works v. Brennan*, 417 U.S. 188 (1974).

10. The plaintiff may be an individual or class who can directly file suit, or an aggrieved employee can file a complaint of an EPA violation with the EEOC, which will investigate and file a lawsuit, if necessary, on the individual's behalf. Until 1979, when the EEOC was given enforcement of the EPA, suits were filed by the Secretary of Labor, the Wage-Hour Division of the Department of Labor having had enforcement powers.

11. Id. at 195-197.

12. See: Kanowitz, "Sex-Based Discrimination in American Law III, Title VII of the 1964 Civil Rights Act and the Equal Pay Act of 1963," 20 *Hastings Law Journal*

305, 311 (1973). A congressman from Virginia, an opponent of the bill, introduced the Smith Amendment, which added sex as a prohibited basis of discrimination. Some supporters of the bill opposed the amendment, arguing that it was a diversionary tactic that would weaken the whole. But other supporters of the bill, women representatives, endorsed the idea. For a discussion of this issue by the courts, see: *Gerlach v. Michigan Bell Telephone Co.*, 501 F. Supp. 1300 (1980), at 1309-1310.

13. Nothing in the language of Title VII, however, limits its reach to women, and men who feel aggrieved by affirmative action, for example, have brought suit under Title VII.

14. Id. at §2000e-2 (a) (1-2). Similar restrictions are imposed on employment agencies, labor organizations, and joint labor-management committees that control apprenticeship or other training programs. Exceptions are made to these broad prohibitions to allow employers (and the other covered groups) to hire or classify employees based on religion, sex, or national origin—but not race or color—in "those certain instances where religion, sex, or national origin is a bona fide occupational qualification reasonably necessary to the normal operation of that particular business or enterprise." (Naturally, this has resulted in much judicial disputation about what constitutes a "bona fide occupational qualification" and what is "reasonably necessary" to normal business operations.)

An exception is made, also, to allow schools, colleges, and universities to hire and employ employees of a particular religion if the institution is owned, controlled, or managed by a particular religion.

Other exceptions are permitted: for measures taken against members of the Communist party; for restrictions imposed by national security; for employment practices on Indian reservations; for employers to administer and act upon the results of professionally developed ability tests provided that they are not intended, designed, or used to discriminate against the protected groups; and one other exception of more relevance to our topic that will be discussed in the text. (See §2000e-2 for the text of these exceptions.)

One other exception is worthy of special note; this one seemingly states that it was the intent of Congress not to impose an obligation on employers to actively go out and give preferential treatment to any individual or group. I say "seemingly" because this has been a bone of contention in affirmative action cases. What is clear, at least to me, is that affirmative action as imposed on federal contractors by Executive Order 11246 (signed by President Johnson on September 24, 1965) is antithetical to the language and intent of Congress in Title VII. Given that federal contractors are defined so broadly as to include any business that sells over $10,000 in goods and services to the federal government within a year, this Executive Order effectively mandated affirmative action for every business but the most minuscule. Title VII's relevant portion reads as follows:

> Sec. 703(j) Nothing contained in this title shall be interpreted to require any employer, employment agency, labor organization, or joint labor-management committee subject to this title to grant preferential treatment to any individual or to any group because of the race, color, religion, sex, or national origin of such individual or group on account of an imbalance which may exist with respect to the total number or percentage of persons of any race, color, religion, sex, or national origin employed by any employer, referred or classified for employment by any employment agency or labor organization, admitted to, or employed in, any apprenticeship or other training

program, in comparison with the total number or percentage of persons of such race, color, religion, sex, or national origin in any community, State, section, or other area, or in the available work force in any community, State, section, or other area.

Despite this language, which seems clear enough, courts and the EEOC interpretation have agreed that statistical inferences based on comparing minorities (or other protected groups) in a business with their representation in the community can be used to establish a prima facie case of discrimination.

15. EEOC Interpretations of the Equal Pay Act, August 20, 1986, 51 FR 29819, §1620.27.
16. For some cases that heavily employ such analysis see: *Sobel v. Yeshiva University*, 32 FEP Cases 154 (DC NY 1983); *Coser v. Moore*, 36 FEP Cases 48 (DC NY, 1983), affirmed 40 FEP Cases 195 (CA 2, 1984); *Wilkins v. University of Houston*, 27 FEP Cases 1199 (CA 5, 1981); *Bazemore v. Friday*, 41 FEP Cases 92 (U.S. Sup. Ct., 1986).
17. Title VIII at §2000e-2(h).
18. The wording does not correspond exactly: Title VII inserts "or different locations," but this is captured in the EPA by the stipulation that the Act only covers work in the same "establishment." What is missing from Title VII is the EPA's fourth defense which covers "a differential based on any other factor other than sex."
19. For some early—pre-*Gunther v. County of Washington*—cases bearing on the interpretation of the Bennett Amendment see: *Electrical Workers, IUE v. Westinghouse Electric Corp.*, 23 FEP Cases 588 (CA3, 1980), in which the appeals court held that the Bennett Amendment merely incorporates into Title VII the four exceptions permitted under the Equal Pay Act; and reaching the opposite result: *Gerlach v. Michigan Bell Telephone Co.*, 24 FEP Cases 69 (DC Mich, 1980). In *Gerlach* the court held that the Bennett Amendment is not intended to limit Title VII sex-based wage discrimination claims to only those cognizable under the EPA.
20. See for example: *Craik v. Minnesota Univerrsity* (CA 8 1984), 34 FEP Cases 649; *Melani v. New York City Bd. of Higher Education* (DC Ny 1983), 31 FEP Cases 648; *Sobel v. Yeshiva Univ.* (DC NY 1983) 32 FEP Cases 154.
21. See for example: *AFSCME v. Nassau County, N.Y.* (DC NY 1983) 37 FEP Cases 1424; *Brooks v. Ashtabula County Welfare Dept.* (CA 6 1983) 32 FEP Cases 1368; *Morqado v. Birmingham-Jefferson County Civil Defense Corps* (CA 11 1983) 32 FEP Cases 12.
22. See for example: *Odomes v. Nucare, Inc.* (CA 6 1981) 26 FEP Cases 317; *Lemons v. City & County of Denver* (CA 10 1980) 27 FEP Cases 959; *Briggs v. City of Madison* (DC Wis 1982) 32 FEP Cases 739.
23. See for example: *Spaulding v. Washington; Coser v. Moore* (DC NY 1983) 36 FEP Cases 48.
24. See for example: *Jurich v. Mahoning County* (DC Ohio 1983) 32 FEP Cases 1274; *Gunther v. County of Washington; Ruffin v. County of Los Angeles* (CA 9 1979) 21 FEP Cases 386.
25. See for example: *Stastny v. Southern Bell Telephone Co.* (CA 4 1980) 23 FEP Cases 665; *Champion v. Pacific Telephone & Telegraph Co.* (DC Mich 1980) 21 FEP Cases 1058; *Gerlach v. Michigan Bell Telephone Co.* (DC Mich 1980) 24 FEP Cases 69.

26. See for example: *Oakes v. City of Fairhope, Ala.* (DC Ala 1981) 28 FEP Cases 74.
27. Joy Ann Grune, "Pay Equity is a Necessary Remedy for Wage Discrimination," in *Comparable Worth: Issue for the 80s*, A Consultation of the U.S. Commission on Civil Rights (June 6-7, 1984), Volume 1, p. 166.
28. *Christensen v. State of Iowa*, 563 F.2d 353 (1977).
29. Id. at 354.
30. *McDonnell Douglas Corp. v. Green*, 411 U.S. 792, 800 (1973).
31. *Christensen v. State of Iowa*, at 356.
32. 17 FEP Cases 907 (1978); and 620 F. 2d 228 (1980) for the appeals court decision.
33. The latter (42 U.S.C. Sec. 1983) states that:

> Every person who, under color of any statute, ordinance, regulation, custom or usage, of any State or Territory, subjects, or causes to be subjected, any citizen of the United States or other person within the jurisdiction thereof to the deprivation of any rights, privileges, or immunities secured by the Constitution and laws, shall be liable to the party injured in an action at law, suit in equity, or other proper proceeding for redress. . . .

34. *Lemons*, 17 FEP Cases 907, at 906-907.
35. Id. at 908-909.
36. Id. at 909.
37. Id. at 914.
38. Other pre-*Gunther* cases that rejected the comparable worth concept include: *Pantchenko v. C.B. Dolge Co.*, 18 FEP Cases 686 (D. Conn. 1977), *affirmed in part and reversed and remanded in part on other grounds*, 581 F. 2d 1052 (2d Cir. 1978); *Gerlach v. Michigan Bell Telephone Co.*, 501 F. Supp. 1300 (E. D. Mich. 1980).
   In this case, Judge Patricia Boyle did not seem hostile to the comparable worth standard; in fact she stated that: "the Court wholeheartedly concurs in the observation that the advancement of women and minorities will not be assured until employers pay all persons according to their value to the enterprise."
   However, after a meticulous examination of the congressional history on Title VII and the Equal Pay Act and the judicial precedents, she could find no legislative intent to give the courts the power to make judgments about the relative worth of different jobs. (at 1321); *IUE v. Westinghouse Electric Corp.*, 17 FEP Cases 16 (N.D. W. Va. 1977); and *IUE v. Westinghouse Electric Corp.*, 631 F. 2d 1094 (1980).
39. *Fitzgerald v. Sirloin Stockade*, 624 F. 2d 945 (10th Cir. 1980).
40. *Gunther v. County of Washington*, 602 F. 882 (9th Cir. 1979).
41. Id. at 891.
42. *IUE v. Westinghouse Electric Corp.*, 631 F. 2d 1094 (1980).
43. *County of Washington v. Gunther*, 452 U.S. 161 (1981).
44. For commentaries on *Gunther*, see: Comment, "Civil Rights—Employment Discrimination—Sex Based Compensation Discrimination," 28 *N.Y.L. Sch. L. Rev.* 149 (1983); Janice R. Bellace, "Comparable Worth: Proving Sex-Based Wage Discrimination," 69 *Iowa L Rev.* 855 (1984); Judith Anne Pauley, "The Exception Swallows the Rule: Market Conditions as a 'Factor Other than Sex' in Title VII Disparate Impact Litigation," 86 *W. Vir. L. Rev.* 165 (1983); Charles

Waldauer, "The Non-Comparability of the Comparable Worth Doctrine: An Inappropriate Standard for Determining Sex Discrimination in Pay," 3 *Population Research and Policy Review* 141 (1984); Sandra Hurd, Paula Murray, Bill Shaw, "Comparable Worth: A Legal and Ethical Analysis," 22 *American Business L.J.* 417 (1984).

45. *County of Washington v. Gunther*, at 166.
46. Id. at 167 n. 8.
47. Id. at 168.
48. Id. at 178-179.
49. Id. at 181.
50. Id.
51. By permissible reason, I mean one of the four affirmative defenses incorporated into Title VII by the Bennett Amendment.
52. *County of Washington v. Gunther*, Rehnquist dissent, at 182.
53. Id. at 189. The doctrine is known as in pari materia.
54. Id. at 183.
55. *AFSCME v. Washington*, 578 F. Supp. 846 (1983).
56. Id. at 861.
57. These figures are based on a subsequent study in 1984; Washington Department of Personnel, as quoted in "Pay Equity Fight to Continue," *USA Today*, September 6, 1985, p. 6A.
58. *AFSCME v. Washington*, at 861.
59. *Dothard v. Rawlinson*, 433 U.S. 321, 328-329 (1977).
60. *Griggs v. Duke Power Co.*, 401 U.S. 424, 430-431 (1971).
61. *Harriss v. Pan American World Airways, Inc.*, 649 F. 2d 670, 674 (9th Cir. 1980). What these cases indicate is that disparate impact has been applied to Section 703(a) (2) claims, but rarely to compensation claims under Section 703(a) (1). Section 703(a) (2) reads in relevant part:

> It shall be an unlawful employment practice for an employer—to limit, segregate, or classify his employees or applicants for employment in any way which would deprive or tend to deprive any individual of employment opportunities . . . because of such individual's . . . sex . . .

62. *International Brotherhood of Teamsters v. United States*, 431 U.S. 324, 335 n. 15 (1977).
63. *McDonnell Douglass Corp. V. Green*, 411 U.S 792 (1973).
64. As Judge Tanner related it in *AFSCME*, circumstantial evidence that can prove intentional discrimination includes:

> the historical context out of which the challenged practices arise; obstacles confronting applicants and/or employees; subjective employment practices utilized by the Defendant resulting in a pattern disfavoring females; the foreseeable adverse impact of those practices; the increase in pay to the Plaintiffs since filing of the instant suit; discriminatory treatment in other areas of employment; and, perhaps most telling, recognition of disparate treatment by responsible state officials.

> *AFSCME v. Washington*, at 858.

65. Id. at 856, as quoted from *Country of Washington v. Gunther*, at 161.
66. Id. at 864.

67. Id. at 865.
68. Id. at 868 n. 17.
69. *AFSCME v. State of Washington*, 770 F. 2d 1401, 1408 (1985).
70. Id.
71. Id. at 1407.
72. *Spaulding v. University of Washington*, 35 FEP Cases 217 (1984), which affirmed the district court, 35 FEP Cases 168 (1981). The appeals court wrote:

> We cannot manageably apply the [disparate] impact model when the kernel of the plaintiff's theory is comparable worth. . . . Every employer constrained by market forces must consider market values in setting his labor costs. Naturally, market prices are inherently job-related, although the market may embody social judgments as to the worth of some jobs. Employers relying on the market are, to that extent, "pricetakers." They deal with the market as a given, and do not meaningfully have a "policy" about it in the relevant Title VII sense. (Id. at 232.)

The court, too, rejected the plaintiffs' disparate treatment contention.
The case was brought by women faculty members at the University of Washington who contended that the university violated the Equal Pay Act by paying them less than men in other divisions of the school. The district court rejected this, finding that they had not shown that their work was substantially equal to that of the men. They, further, argued that even if they could not prove equality of work, under the *Gunther* ruling they could make out a case of sex-based wage discrimination in violation of Title VII, under both the disparate impact and disparate treatment models.
73. "State of Washington Reaches Comparable Worth Agreement," UPI, January 2, 1986.
74. For an account of AFSCME's numerous activities on the comparable worth front, see the by-now-slightly-outdated: *Winning the Fight for Pay Equity, American Federation of State, County and Municipal Employees, AFL-CIO*, 1984.
75. *American Nurses Association v. State of Illinois*, 40 FEP Cases 245 (1986).
76. Id. at 246.
77. Id. at 247.
78. Id. at 255.
79. Id. at 249.
80. *Pennsylvania Nurses Association v. Commonwealth of Pennsylvania*, USDC, MPa, Case No. CV-86-1586, filed Nov. 7, 1986. For a brief article on this case, see: "Job and Pay Structure Suit," *Fair Employment Practices*, November 27, 1986.
81. 109 Cong. Rec. 9197 (1963), as quoted in *County of Washington v. Gunther*, Rehnquist dissent, at 187. For two other cases that exhaustively examine the legislative history, see: *Gerlach v. Michigan Bell Telephone* and *IUE v. Westinghouse Electric Co.*.
82. 110 Cong. Rec. 7217 (1964), as quoted in Rehnquist's *Gunther* dissent, at 191.
83. 110 Cong. Rec. 13647 (1964), and Id. at 193.
84. 111 Cong. Rec. 13359 (1965); and Id. at 194.
85. *County of Washington v. Gunther*, at 176.
86. Id. at 170, quoting their earlier decision in *Griggs v. Duke Power Co.*, 401 U.S. 424, 431 (1971).

87. Donald J. Treiman and Heidi I. Hartmann, eds., *Women, Work, and Wages* (Washington, D.C.: National Academy Press, 1981), p. x.
88. Id. at 10.
89. Id. at 67.
90. The Carter era revisions would have revised Section 60-20.5 of the code to read: (a) *Wages*. The contractor's wage schedules must not be related to or based on the sex of the employees.

    While the more obvious cases of discrimination exist where employees of different sexes are paid different wages on jobs which require substantially equal skill, effort and responsibility and are performed under similar working conditions, compensation practices with respect to any jobs where males or females are concentrated will be scrutinized closely to assure that sex has played no role in setting of levels of pay.
91. Case. No. 85-8, June 17, 1985, 37 *FEP Cases* 1889.
92. Id. at 1891.
93. Id. at 1892.
94. "Equal Pay is not Needed for Jobs of Comparable Worth, U.S. Says," *New York Times*, June 18, 1985.
95. "Use of Comparable-Worth Idea to Fight Job Sex Bias Opposed by Rights Panel," *The Wall Street Journal*, April 12, 1985.
96. "Rights Panel Rejects Comparable Worth," UPI, April 12, 1985.
97. Most of the comparable worth activity has been generated since 1981. However, fourteen states had language in their equal pay laws that prohibited unequal compensation rates for 'comparable work' or 'work of comparable character' before the 1980s. Arkansas, Georgia, Idaho, Kentucky, Maine, North Dakota, Oklahoma, South Dakota, and Tennessee, prohibit unequal pay on a comparable work standard, while Alaska, Maryland, Massachusetts, Oregon, and West Virginia employ the comparable character criterion. In almost all of these states, the standard of 'comparability' applies to public and also to private employees. But these old statutes do not define methods for determining comparability or assessing the extent of sexual discrimination. The new-style legislation of the 1980s has, in many states, given teeth to these otherwise rather undefined pronouncements. See: *PAY EQUITY AND COMPARABLE WORTH*, a BNA Special Report, pp. 55-56.

    These old pay equity statutes were typically enacted in the 1960s (e.g., Georgia's in 1966; Idaho's in 1969; Oklahoma's in 1965; although Arkansas's act was enacted in 1955) and they mirror pretty closely the Federal Equal Pay Act standards, with similar exceptions for seniority, merit pay, and other nondiscriminatory differences. Oklahoma's language is typical:

    > It shall be unlawful for any employer within the state of Oklahoma to wilfully pay wages to women employees at a rate less than the rate at which he pays any employee of the opposite sex for comparable work on jobs which have comparable requirements relating to skill, effort and responsibility, except where such payment is made pursuant to a seniority system; a merit system; a system which measures earnings by a quantity or quality of production; or a differential based on any factor other than sex. (Oklahoma Equal Pay Act, H.B. 840, L. 1965)

    Despite the "comparability" language in these statutes, their interpretation, with very few exceptions, has been no different from the "equal pay for equal work'' standard of the Equal Pay Act of 1963. But, in the 1980s, these old pay equity statutes have not been entirely useless to the comparable worth cause. In Alaska, the State Commission for Human Rights used equal pay language in its Human Rights Law to decide that the state had violated the law by paying public health nurses, mostly women, less than an all-male crew of physicians' assistants. The commission determined that the work of each group was of 'comparable character'. *Alaska State Commission for Human Rights v. State of Alaska*, Alaska State Commission for Human Rights, Case No. D-79-0724-188-E, Nov. 15, 1985. The relevant portion of the Alaska Human Rights Law (Sec. 18.80.220 (5)) reads as follows:

> It is unlawful for an employer to discriminate in the payment of wages as between the sexes, or to employ a female in an occupation in this state at a salary or wage rate less than that paid to a male employee for work of comparable character or work in the same operation, business or type of work in the same locality.

All but ten states have enacted equal pay acts, with most (other than the fourteen discussed above) mirroring the federal equal pay standard, although there are some statutes with even narrower language than equal pay for equal work, e.g., Arizona's act:

> No employer shall pay any person in his employ at wag. ,ates less than the rate paid to employees of the opposite sex in the same establishment for the same classification of work . . .
>
> (Arizona Revised Statutes, Article 6.1, Ch. 2, Title 23, Sec. 23-341.)

Other states use language that simply bans differences in pay based on sex, e.g., Connecticut:

> No employer shall discriminate in the amount of compensation paid to any employee solely on the basis of sex. . . . (Title 31, Sec. 58, Connecticut General Statutes)

98. The ten states with comparable worth pay policies are: Hawaii, Iowa, Maine, Michigan, Minnesota, Montana, Ohio, Oregon, Washington, Wisconsin. These ten have conducted comparable worth studies, as have an additional eighteen states: Arizona, California, Illinois, Indiana, Kansas, Kentucky, Louisiana, Maryland, Massachusetts, Nebraska, New Jersey, New Mexico, New York, North Carolina, Rhode Island, Vermont, West Virginia, Wyoming. This GAO report seems to be the most comprehensive and up-to-date study available, but there are differences between this report and others. In California, for example, the personnel officials said they could not say whether the state had a pay equity policy or not, as it may be superceded by collective bargaining, yet such a policy was seemingly adopted in 1981. See: *Pay Equity: Status of State Activities*, General Accounting Office, GAO/GGD-86-141/BR, September 19, 1986. Two states did not report information to the GAO: Alabama and Pennsylvania. The latter has considered comparable worth legislation but has not succeeded in passing a bill. See also: Alice L. Ahmuty, ''Summary of Pay Equity/Comparable Worth Activities by State Governments,'' Congressional Research Service, The Library of Congress, 85-615 E, March 12, 1985.

99. Ronnie Steinberg, " 'A Want of Harmony': Perspectives of Wage Discrimination and Comparable Worth," in Helen Remick ed., *Comparable Worth and Wage Discrimination* (Philadelphia: Temple University Press, 1984), p. 21.
100. "Ohio Panel Favors 'Comparable Worth' Law," UPI, September 6, 1984.
101. "In Minnesota, 'Pay Equity' Passes Test, but Foes See Trouble Ahead," *The Wall Street Journal*, May 10, 1985.
102. Nina Rothchild, "Overview of Pay Initiatives, 1974-1984," *Comparable Worth: Issue for the 80s*, pp. 122-125.
103. "In Minnesota, 'Pay Equity' Passes Test."
104. For a fuller discussion see: Ronnie Steinberg, " 'A Want of Harmony,' " p. 15.
105. This discussion is drawn from: Janice R. Bellace, "A Foreign Perspective," in *Comparable Worth: Issues and Alternatives*, E. Robert Livernash, ed. (Washington, D.C.: Equal Employment Advisory Council, 2nd ed. 1984), pp. 140-141. Bellace says the "equal value" language came from the 1919 Peace Treaty that ended World War I and established the ILO. She could find no reason to think the author of the phrase, Lord Balfour, intended anything beyond equal pay for substantially similar work. She saw a few hints of comparable worth intent in some of the statements made during the 1951 session of the convention, but most statements assumed the expression meant "equal pay for equal work." Officially, she adds, the ILO understands the equal pay formulation as broader than equal pay for similar work.
106. Again, this discussion is drawn from Bellace's "A Foreign Perspective," pp. 143-144.
107. Rita Cadieux, "Canada's Equal Pay for Work of Equal Value Law," in *Comparable Worth & Wage Discrimination*, pp. 173-196.
108. Id. at 177.
109. This discussion of the Canadian equal pay standard has been drawn from Rita Cadieux, "Canada's Equal Pay for Work of Equal Value Law."
110. This discussion of the pay equity situation in Australia was drawn from the following sources: Bellace, "A Foreign Perspective"; R.G. Gregory, P. McMahon, B. Whittingham, "Women in the Australian Labor Force: Trends, Causes, and Consequences," 3 *Journal of Labor Economics* §293 (1985); and R.G. Gregory and R.C. Duncan, "Segmented Labor Market Theories and the Australian Experience of Equal Pay for Women," 3 *Journal Post-Keynesian Economy* 403 (1981).

4

Resolving the Debate: Some Philosophical Considerations

As we have seen in previous chapters, both the comparable worth opponents and the judges who have been reluctant to read a comparable worth remedy into Title VII base their opposition to the concept essentially on economic grounds. The critics argue that imposing comparable worth would have these deleterious economic consequences: it would be far too costly; it would cause economic disruption in the form of inflation, unemployment, and an inability to compete on international markets; and, more generally, it would undermine our free-market system.

The case the opponents make against comparable worth is *prima facie* quite persuasive, and the question then becomes: Can the comparable worth advocates surmount that case by rebutting the essential charges? After a careful examination of the arguments of both sides, I conclude that they cannot. While I am sympathetic to the goals that have prompted many people to support comparable worth—women's equality in the work place and a society free of invidious discrimination—comparable worth is not the appropriate remedy.

Comparable worth's opponents score their most telling blows against the notion that value can be objectively measured and that job evaluations can provide the tool for performing such measurements and, ultimately, for comparing radically dissimilar jobs. I will treat at greater length the subject of objective value below, but for now what ought to be clear about job evaluations is that they are highly subjective. Norman Willis, one of the most active consultants on comparable worth job evaluations, conceded as much after the initial decision in *AFSCME v. Washington*, when he expressed concern that any one expert's scheme could be mandated by law.

Others sympathetic to comparable worth—such as Paul Weiler and the Treiman and Hartmann committee—also acknowledge this seemingly insoluble problem of subjectivity in job evaluations. Job evaluators have succumbed to pressure from unions to modify their conclusions, as occurred in Maryland, with the evaluators finding no discrimination initially, and then discovering the opposite under intense persuasion by the unions. Job evaluations as they have been conducted in the states involve a great deal of bargaining between examiners who do not agree about point awards and the weighing of various factors, and the committees conducting these studies have been dominated by those predisposed to comparable worth, and hence predisposed toward discerning discrimination against female-dominated jobs.

The attempt by supporters to devise techniques for refining job evaluations to e¹˙ ₋inate alleged market discrimination only seems to exacerbate the proble₋ ₋ of arbitrariness. Cut off from the check of correspondence to prevailing market rates for benchmark jobs, comparable worth evaluations provide room for imposing any kind of values the examiners might bring to the study.

But what about the suggestions for eliminating this problem of evaluator bias? In a scheme suggested by Treiman and Hartmann and pursued by Paul Weiler, benchmark jobs for men would be studied in a given firm to find the "implicit value" system behind them, and then the same values would be applied to the female jobs. Thus, these conditional supporters of comparable worth claim, evaluators would not be imposing their own values, but would only take the values of the firm and ensure that they be consistently applied and that discrimination against women be eliminated.

Upon examination, this suggestion seems to be grounded on erroneous assumptions. Since all prices are set in markets, including the price of the commodity labor, employers have minimal control over the prices they pay for particular kinds of labor. Thus, to reconstruct a hidden agenda of implicit values from the salaries an employer actually pays to men is to try to construct a rational pattern out of phenomena that are, to all intents and purposes, random occurrences. Not that they are truly random, but the factors that determine them are so numerous, and the effect on them of any one employer so trivial, that they could just as well be considered random: as givens. Most employers are price takers, not price makers, when it comes to the wages offered particular kinds of labor. So to impute discrimination to an employer simply for following market prices of labor would be arbitrary in the extreme, in the absence of any more direct proof of discriminatory intent or behavior.

Thus, even in its most narrow application—to a single firm—and with a fairly sophisticated attempt to limit evaluator subjectivity, job evaluations divorced from market prices appear to be hopelessly defective devices. They will not, except by a series of arbitrary decisions, arrive at comparisons that can be accepted by society as proof of discrimination and as grounds for remediation. Since these are the two purposes the comparable worth supporters take job evaluations to perform, their failure to resolve the problem of subjectivity is damning, indeed. Why forsake the market, one wonders, for comparable worth job evaluations when the latter are irremediably value laden and when each evaluator using his own system arrives at different results.

At this point, it would be useful to step back from the heat of the debate and examine in greater detail some of the assumptions underlying comparable worth. Comparable worth will be seen to depend on some rather dubious assumptions and to embrace a view of equality that is at odds with our American tradition, unpersuasive as an ideal, and incapable of being put into practice without chaotic results.

Assumptions

Comparable Worth and Intrinsic Value

When the critics charge that comparable worth depends on a notion of intrinsic value that can be measured on an objective scale, they have identified a fundamental misconception that underpins the case for imposing comparable worth. Intrinsic or objective value theories are by no means new. St. Thomas Aquinas and other Medieval theorists endorsed a notion of "just price," and this intrinsic-value view was exemplified in the guild system, which set prices not only for the labor of guild members but also for their products.

The classical economists of the nineteenth century, as well as Karl Marx, argued for an objective theory of value, the labor theory. Normally, the classical economists contended, the price of commodities depends upon the amount of labor spent in bringing them to market. Market forces, such as scarcity or a temporary shift in demand, could modify this price, so that the market price would fluctuate around this norm.

The theory had numerous, glaring problems. The principal one was that it could not explain everyday market phenomena. For example, why is the price of water negligible while the price of diamonds is substantial? Water has great use value to sustain life, while diamonds have only a frivolous, ornamental function. The labor theory of value fell in the late nineteenth century to a more sophisticated theory, one that did not claim that value was derived from any objective quality, but rather that value depended upon the subjective judgments of people in the marketplace, and the supply of the good in question.

This marginal utility theory of value had several noteworthy advantages over its objective, labor-theory competitor. It solved the water-diamond "paradox." Diamonds are priced higher than water because people are willing to pay more for them. Diamonds are relatively scarce, compared with water, hence the marginal unit of diamonds commands a higher price than the marginal unit of water. If water suddenly became scarce, people would value it more highly and be willing to pay more to acquire it, and its price would rise.

The marginal theory also explained what the labor theory could not; that is, how prices are set for everyday commodities in the market. The new theory could explain why misdirected labor time—that is, time spent producing widgets no one wants—would command no equivalent compensation in the marketplace; it could explain why commodities embodying the same labor time did not appear to trade equally on the market.

Despite Marx's abhorrence of this fact, labor power is as much a commodity as anything else. The price of any particular kind of labor is set by the same criteria as any other good. The market price equates supply and demand; each laborer is paid the equivalent of his marginal productivity, his contribution to the enterprise. Marginal utility theory, thus, overcame another problem inherent in a labor theory of value: that every factor of production—labor, land, entrepreneurship—required a different theory to explain how its price was set.

Now, what bearing does all of this have on comparable worth? Comparable worth shares with the labor theory of value a desire to discover some objective characteristics of worth or value apart from the valuations in the marketplace derived from the choices of actual buyers. For comparable worth, the hours of labor embodied in a thing no longer set its value, but rather, the value of labor itself can be determined by assessing its components: knowledge, skills, mental demands, accountability, working conditions.

What comparable worth's proponents are searching for is some identifiable, objective qualities that are transferable from job to job and that everyone could, at least theoretically, agree upon. But are they not searching in vain? The perpetual squabbles among evaluators performing studies in the states, the instructions of consultants to the evaluation committees that they should go with their gut instincts in assessing points, and the reevaluations that go on once the scores have been assembled are empirical evidence of a problem that really lies on the theoretical level.

If there is no intrinsic value to a job, then it cannot be measured. Let us look at the wage-setting process as it unfolds in the market to see what the price of labor means, if it does not mean a measurement of intrinsic value.

A job has value to someone who creates it and is willing to pay someone to do it. The price of that job is set in the labor market, which is nothing more than an arena for satisfying the demands for labor of various sorts by numerous employers. What an employer is willing to pay for the type of labor he needs depends on his assessment of what that labor can contribute to the ultimate product and what price he thinks those products will command in the market. The labor market is an impersonal process. In most cases, employers and potential employees do not know each other before the process is begun. It is impersonal in another way, also. No individual employer can exercise much influence over the price of labor of the kind he needs. Only in the rarest of cases, where no alternative employers are available to willing workers, will any one employer have much of an impact on the overall job market. Such influence characterizes centrally planned, government-owned economies much more than it does market economies. To the extent that markets are distorted by government-imposed monopolies or cartels, the actual market departs from the theoretical one.

The supporters of comparable worth consider this view of the market naive. Rather, they say, markets are dominated by monopolies that dictate wages to workers who by-and-large have no other options. The problem with this argument is that it is simply not true that the labor market in the United States is largely dominated by monopolies. What has characterized capitalist economies since the Industrial Revolution is precisely the options that workers have, the fluidity of labor markets, and the ever-changing possibilities the market creates. Unlike the Middle Ages, where workers' options were essentially limited to following the paternal occupation and where class status was very nearly immutable, capitalism presents workers with a plethora of options.

Indeed, this kaleidoscopic choice is precisely the aspect of capitalism to which its early opponents, both of the socialist and patriarchal variety, most vehemently objected. Where monopolies do exist, they are usually the result of governmental interference, for example, by grants of monopoly, and not by the action of the marketplace. While temporary monopolies may arise in a free market, they tend not to last, as upstart companies and their new technology eventually upset the staid "monopolists."

To return to our description of the labor market, if an employer, through discriminatory motivation or any other reason, wishes to pay less than the prevailing wage for a certain kind of labor, one of three things will normally happen. He will get no takers. He will get fewer takers than he needs. Or the quality of the applicant pool will be lower than the job requires. Conversely, if he wishes to pay more, he will get many applicants and some of them will be of higher quality than normal in that job classification.

In the former case, the employer jeopardizes his business by presumably making his products less marketable and his operation less efficient; in the latter case, the employer may benefit his business if his more skilled employees produce more products or a better product that the consumers are willing to pay a higher price to acquire. The consumer, however, may not be willing, and then the business would be jeopardized.

Thus, employers are, in the normal case, pretty much tied to paying prevailing market wages. Those employers who discriminate for irrelevant reasons—like race, sex, religion—put themselves at a competitive disadvantage by restricting the pool of labor from which they can select workers. If discrimination against blacks or women, for example, were prevalent in the society, the price of such labor would be lower than for comparable labor provided by members of other groups. Those employers willing to hire the despised will benefit from lower prices for their labor and will enjoy a competitive edge. In the absence of laws enshrined by governments to perpetuate discrimination, the market should correct for it over time by penalizing discriminatory employers and rewarding the others. Eventually, the wages of the discriminated will rise.

If jobs have no intrinsic worth, then the comparable worth position has been severely wounded, for it bases its case on precisely such an assumption. What I have argued is that jobs have no intrinsic value within the context of a market economy. Now, that is an important caveat. A competing system, one that sets the prices for all goods, services, and labor by a central planning agency could provide an alternative framework to the market. But would the price of various types of labor be objectively set in such a system? All we could say is that the planners would tell everyone else what each job was worth. Via job evaluations, direct flashes of insight, or whatever methodology they chose, the wages of labor would be set and everyone would abide by those directives. One might call such a system objective in the sense that departures from the assigned wages might be punishable, but using the term in the way we normally do, it seems like rampant subjectivism. As John Stuart Mill wrote a century ago:

> A fixed rule, like that of equality, might be acquiesced in, and so might chance, or an external necessity; but that a handful of human beings should weight everybody in the balance, and give more to one and less to another at their *sole* pleasure and judgment, would not be borne unless from persons believed to be more than men, and backed by supernatural terrors.[1]

F. A. Hayek argued, in *The Road to Serfdom*, that planning for security—the aim of central planners—is incompatible with freedom of choice in employment. He wrote:

> This demand for security is thus another form of the demand for a just remuneration—a remuneration commensurate with the subjective merits and not with the objective results of a man's efforts. This kind of security or justice seems irreconcilable with freedom to choose one's employment.[2]

It is rather intriguing to observe the extent to which our use of language has been transmuted since he wrote those words in 1944. Where Hayek saw subjectivity in such things as the years of schooling or training of workers, the comparable worth forces see objectivity; where he saw objectivity in the salaries actually received in the market, they see subjectivity, arbitrariness, and discrimination.

Hayek's great insight lies in his identification of a desire by some—and he was arguing against advocates of socialistic central planning and not comparable worth, but the argument seems to be as good against the latter—to correct the perceived injustices of the market by human devices. Namely, by trying to fix security for one group after another. The end result of such a process, he thought, is the elimination of freedom, while the more immediate result is the impoverishment of those groups without enough clout to secure benefits from the state.

But I take it that this kind of command economy, which Hayek argued so persuasively against, is not really what the comparable worth supporters want. Most of them, leaving aside the most radical who embrace socialism or Marxism, contend that they do not wish to replace the market, only to make it fairer to women. They profess to see nothing radical about their chosen tool, only a natural progression from the equal opportunity laws we already have on the books. But if they do not wish to abandon the market, they must somehow surmount the argument that jobs do not have intrinsic worth or objective value within the market context. They have not done so, because it is impossible to understand the market and to argue for objective value. If they cannot make the argument, they are left with no choice, logically, but to embrace central planning, in which the only form of "objectivity" would be the decrees of those in authority; or, as George Orwell might have said: a world in which objectivity equals subjectivity.

Another problem with this quest for objective value or worth is that it confuses moral language with economic language. Surely, economists talk about value: they mean by the value of a commodity what it will trade for at any particular time in the marketplace. There is nothing mysterious, no essence that lies buried beneath this market value (at least since the labor theory of value was abandoned).

What the comparable worth people mean by value is something essential to any particular type of labor. They are looking for some higher order moral principle that, irrespective of the market, can compare the work of the plumber to the tree-trimmer to the grocer to the secretary to the nurse. Within our society, there is no agreement about higher order moral principles: about what contributes to the good life; what activities are worthy of pursuit in their own right; what kinds of behavior contribute to the welfare of society. How can we expect individuals in society to agree about how particular jobs contribute to ends, when those ends themselves are in dispute?

Wouldn't it be an unpleasant world if people did agree about values, if those values could be objectively measured as they were exemplified in different jobs, and if they were paid accordingly? Then, if Michael Jackson earned a million dollars for each performance while an emergency room nurse received $20 for her work during the same two hours, we would know that he was really worth 50,000 times as much as she; that is, that society valued her contribution so very much less. We would know, simply by the salary paid to each person in such a society, exactly what his social contribution and, presumably, his social status was. But on a market we cannot even infer that a plumber making $10 an hour is worth more or less to his employer than a teacher who earns the same wage is worth to hers. Such comparisons are vacuous. One's worth, in the moral sense, is not measured in the marketplace by one's wage. Price and salary are economic terms, and they depend upon the available supply and the demand for particular kinds of labor. Value and worth are moral terms, as comparable worth's supporters intend them, and they do not equate well at all with price in the marketplace. Thus, even the market cannot equate the worth (in the moral sense) of one job with another; all it shows is that at any particular time secretaries are paid more or less than zoo keepers.

Any attempt to employ "objective" job assessment criteria must be inherently discretionary. That blanket statement stands unrefuted by the comparable worth camp. I believe it is logically impossible for them to surmount this difficulty: for they cannot find objectivity by appealing to the views of experts who, as human beings, bring their prejudices to any assessment; nor can they find it by abandoning the market and embracing central planning, which is nothing more than personal whims enshrined in decrees. Either way, the judgments of bureaucrats or judges would be forcibly substituted for the assessments of those who are the actual purchasers of labor services. This is unavoidable, since there is no intrinsic value to any job. The impersonal forces of the market would have to be replaced by subjective judgments, by the opinions of "experts." Even if these "experts" were bereft of all tastes—which is, of course, inconceivable—they could not implement a system of objective measurement. Where is the metric? None is to be found. While each person can order his own preferences, these separate preference orders cannot be equated. Similarly, different jobs cannot be equated on any objective scale, at least not until everyone is in agreement about ultimate moral values. Even then, their particular application would be open to differences of opinion.

The comparable worth critics are correct: there is no intrinsic value to any job, and, hence, they can neither be measured nor compared.

Comparable Worth and the Market

Most proponents of comparable worth argue that it is not an alternative to the market, that it is like other correctives to the market that have been instituted by government in recent years. I contend that this is false. Comparable worth, unlike the Equal Pay Act, Title VII, and affirmative action, cannot be grafted onto the market. Rather, the market and comparable worth emanate from two entirely different normative assumptions about individual action.

The market exemplifies the assumption that individual consumers ought to be sovereign, that their desires ought to rule the economy. Comparable worth assumes that individuals ought not be the final arbiters of economic life. Some individuals, rather, should place their judgments above those of the rest of their countrymen. These "experts" will ensure that wage decisions are made on equitable, nonprejudicial grounds.

The Equal Pay Act said to employers that you cannot pay women less than you pay men for the same job. Title VII said to employers that you cannot discriminate in hiring, promotion, compensation, and so forth between men and women. And affirmative action said to employers that you must try to advance women, as historic victims of discrimination, to positions in which they had been under-represented. All of these mandates interfered with employers' rights (and employees' rights, too). All limited employers' freedom. Formerly, an employer could hire whomever he liked, pay whatever he liked, and use any criteria for hiring that he wished.[3]

But comparable worth is different. Instead of employers determining their wage scales by evaluating their demand for a certain type of labor and the supply of it on the market, "expert" boards would have to examine the jobs in each firm or government bureau and set wage scales according to the comparability of different jobs. While most comparable worth advocates do not envision one wage board doing this for the entire economy—as the National War Labor Board tried to do during World War II—it is obvious that some national standards would have to evolve or be imposed, either by legislative act, bureaucratic decree, or judicial interpretation. Without such a universal standard, employers would be left in perpetual limbo about how to stay on the right side of the law: they would hang on each turn of the judicial worm.

Even if there were many boards rather than one, this would still prove problematical on several grounds, in addition to the ones previously raised in the discussion of intrinsic worth. The very reason for having "expert" boards to assess jobs rather than the market is to eliminate subjectivity and, thus, prejudice. But can the boards accomplish this?

As Richard Burr graphically illustrated with his comparisons of state comparable worth studies, they cannot. All people have prejudices, and if that is too harsh a term, all have tastes. Consultants in their comparable worth evaluations have proven themselves systematically more sympathetic to white-collar than blue-collar jobs, to credentials over job experience (thus reversing some of the alleged biases in traditional job evaluations). What is to ensure that a board acts impartially? Will we need another board to assess the fairness of the first, and yet another to judge the fairness of the second. Or, more likely, will we witness appeals courts frequently replacing the judgments of district court judges with their own, and then the Supreme Court every once in a while getting in the act. We seem to be caught in an infinite regress problem, with no theoretical end point short of God and no practical end point short of the Supreme Court.

Furthermore, the institution of a comparable worth scheme nationwide would depend not only on a universal standard and pay boards but, more problematically, on a static view of the economy. Let us suppose comparable worth were put into effect and operated at time t_1 to the satisfaction of its supporters. What would immediately happen at time t_2? A myriad of events would occur to upset the carefully crafted design. Consumer choices, preferences for jobs, availability of resources, and so forth would change. In addition to these causes of change that operate in any economic system, the comparable worth scheme itself would generate market distortions. For example, by raising wages for certain kinds of jobs (that is, those dominated by women), comparable worth would generate a tremendous oversupply of workers for such jobs. But this, presumably, would lead to an undersupply of workers in other jobs. Wages in these understaffed fields would have to rise to attract needed workers. However, such an adjustment would put the female-dominated jobs again at a disadvantage, and their wage rates would have to be increased, again, by the regulators. Thus, more and more economic distortion would be engendered.

To avoid total chaos, this dynamic view of the consequences of comparable-worth-induced market distortions indicates that the comparable worth wage boards, or the consulting firms operating from firm to firm, would have to be a permanent fixture of our economy. As soon as "pay equity" were achieved, it would be upset in the next instant. Thus, the comparable worth evaluations would be a continuous process, constantly disrupting the economy, causing massive uncertainty, instability, and the impossibility of any rational planning on the part of businesses, workers, or consumers. Many workers, in addition, would be disadvantaged because the continuous reevaluations would limit their ability to gain security through long-term contracts. The only way to avoid these natural consequences would be an attempt to freeze the economy. But, of course, this is impossible: wage and price controls only appear to freeze the economy, while the market simply goes underground. Therefore, I conclude that comparable worth cannot be operationalized. As philosopher Robert Nozick pointed out, any attempt to impose one pattern of distribution as the just pattern requires perpetual interferences with human freedom of action.[4]

A moderate supporter of comparable worth might respond to such an argument that she only wants to proceed on a firm-by-firm basis, rather than by imposing a sweeping, national reform. But this would be an unstable solution—as I think many of those who advocate it realize—a slippery slope. Companies forced to adopt comparable worth as a result of suits would be at a competitive disadvantage, as their labor costs would rise and there would be little incentive, except to avoid litigation, for other firms to adopt comparable worth, which would likewise disadvantage them. In the end, comparable worth would have to be a national program; piecemeal action simply will not secure the cooperation of all employers in an effort that runs counter to their self-interest.

Thus, the market and comparable worth seem to be mutually exclusive. Either we have market-set wages or we have wages set by administrative boards and courts. The former has decided advantages, since it is both efficient and voluntaristic. The latter has the twin faults that it cannot be put into operation without producing chaos, and that it replaces individual sovereignty with the opinions of "experts."

Discrimination

Comparable worth proponents believe the market for women's work has been distorted by centuries of discrimination. The market devalues the work of women, and hence it should be supplanted.

The work of June O'Neill and others in demythologizing the wage gap is compelling. It is clear that if women exhibited precisely the same characteristics as men—the same level of education and mix of courses, the same longevity at present employment, the same work force participation levels, and so forth—the "wage gap" would shrink to a "wage pittance" of a few cents, as indeed it has for younger women and single women. The case for massive distortions of the market resulting from discrimination just has not been convincingly made. A gap of 10%, which can be putatively accounted for by other intangible factors like motivation, goals, and family commitments, simply cannot carry the case for revolutionizing our market system.

William R. Beer, a sociologist at Brooklyn College, raises an interesting point in trying to assess how important discrimination is in the lives of women (and blacks, too) in the United States. Why not ask the members of the relevant groups how discrimination has affected their lives. Beer cites a study conducted by *The New York Times*, in November 1983, in which they did precisely that. Three questions were posed: "In the place where you work now, do you think you've ever been discriminated against because you're a woman in terms of salary, responsibility, or promotion?" Seventy-seven percent of the women questioned answered "no." "In other places where you have worked, have you ever been discriminated against because you're a woman?" Seventy-three percent said "no." "Has it ever happened to you, that in seeking work, you applied for a job that interested you, only to learn they wanted to hire a man and not a woman?" Eighty-three percent responded "no." Beer concludes that it is false to suppose that a case can be made for systemic discrimination, although individual instances of such discrimination certainly do arise.[5]

But leaving this aside, there is something else fundamentally flawed about the proponents' line of argument. Comparable worth cannot eliminate discrimination from the labor market, and neither can any other s cheme, including the market. The purpose of any hiring process is precis ely to discriminate. A personnel director does not only look for skills in hiring an applicant. Such intangibles as personality, looks, motivation, and so forth play a factor. Just as any employer discriminates in hiring, so the consulting firms or wage boards would impose their tastes and value judgments.

One kind of discrimination that is particularly invidious is government-imposed discrimination. Apartheid is one example; the policies toward Hungarians in Rumania and Turks in Bulgaria, are others. What makes this kind of discrimination so odious is that it is government-imposed, and hence nearly inescapable. Discrimination in the market is haphazard and usually escapable: one employer may not like women, another doesn't like blacks but doesn't mind women, while most look for the best person to do the job. If you don't like the wages or the conditions in one firm, you can join another or start your own. The comparable worth consulting firms, and what I see as the inevitable wage boards, court-appointed masters, or judicial "wage boards," denote more the apartheid and less the market kind of discrimination. The standards would be government mandated and inescapable, except by leaving the country.

The example of Australia, discussed in the previous chapter, should be a sobering lesson to those who seek to replace market forces with government intervention. The comparable worth enthusiasts often neglect to mention that Australia's adoption of comparable worth took place not in a free-market labor environment, but in one in which labor boards set the minimum wages for every type of labor throughout industry. What the labor board grants the labor board can take away. The Australian labor boards had the power to set women's wages below men's for decades, and now they choose to adopt comparable worth; what next? Those who have the power to discriminate in our favor also have the power to discriminate against us.

But the comparable worth supporters might respond: "We're not trying to eliminate all discrimination, all differences in tastes, but only invidious discrimination." One woman's invidious discrimination, however, is another's free choice. We ought not forget that in our headlong rush to create a discrimination-free society—begun in the early 1960s with the Civil Rights Act and augmented by acts against age discrimination, discrimination against the handicapped, and the pregnant—liberty is being squelched: liberty in the sense of the freedom to associate, to hire whomever one chooses for whatever reason. A potential lawsuit lurks every time an employee is fired, not promoted, not given a raise, and every time an applicant is not hired.

Have we fulfilled the liberal ideal of openness and colorblindness that motivated the framers of the Civil Rights Act of 1964, or rather have we moved closer to a genuinely racist society: one that asks employers to keep tallies on the number of preferred minorities they interview for each available job and threatens them with penalties if the ''goals'' are not met; and one that requires job applicants to fill out forms to identify themselves by race? What would comparable worth do except add another layer of discrimination to the Orwellian attempt to create a discrimination-free society by practicing official discrimination?

Let us discriminate for a time in women's favor until the wage gap disappears, the proponents maintain, and then all will be well and comparable worth can be discarded. If we have learned anything by the experience of the last two and a half decades, it is that one antidiscrimination scheme follows ever closer on the heels of the preceding one. It is a never ending process once favored groups achieve their more-than-equal position, the less favored begin to organize and demand their privileges from the government. In the end, I am afraid, a society emerges that is much more discriminatory, much more conscious of racial, sexual, and religious differences than it ever was before the process began. Comparable worth for women today; minorities tomorrow; and everyone the day after tomorrow. Then, the free market is gone, and along with it economic liberty and consumer sovereignty.

If discrimination—meaning tastes—is irremediable, why should we prefer comparable worth and the discrimination of ''experts'' to the market and the discrimination generated by the free choices of all of us?

Equality of Opportunity v. Equality of Results

The labor market as it currently operates in the United States embodies a conception of equality that political theorists call equality of opportunity. All positions in society ought to be open to everyone, without any artificial barriers of race, religion, nationality, sex, and so forth being placed in anyone's way. Where the actual world departs from this model, government intervenes to guarantee the rights of those who have been discriminated against. While equality of opportunity has its problems—it interferes with personal liberty as adumbrated above—it is preferable to the view of equality embodied in the comparable worth position. Equality of opportunity is the liberal conception enshrined in the Civil Rights Act and its successors.[6]

Equality of results, or some looser variant of it, seems to be the vision embraced by comparable worth's adherents. As I have argued earlier, the attempt to put such a principle into operation (as Nozick argued) is doomed to failure. Life will always intervene to upset the carefully balanced apple cart. Even if this were not so, I do not think equality of results is an appealing moral objective. It is contrary to our tradition, going back to John Locke and the natural law theorists, of treating each person as an individual. Equality of results demands that each person be treated as a component of an organic society; the parts must be rearranged and rewarded so the entire organism will be just.

The comparable worth camp might respond that the foregoing is merely an historical argument about Western traditions and is not in itself compelling. I think it is more than that. It is based upon a realization that individuals are different—they have disparate talents, needs, desires, and tastes. These differences cannot be denied. Any attempt to fit such heterogenous beings into one scheme to judge "worth" would involve a massive amount of paternalism: much more extensive and intrusive than the protective labor laws of the late nineteenth century that the comparable worth people so rightly condemn. If individuals freely hiring on the market and individuals freely offering their services determine that dog catchers are "worth" more than nurses and the comparable worth board or court thinks otherwise, then the wishes of countless employers and workers will count for nothing.

Equality of opportunity is more appealing than equality of results because at least it gives more respect to the wishes of individuals and it just tries to guarantee that the process of selection is in some sense "fair." It does not require making independent assessments of the value to society or to a firm of the work of baseball players, laundresses, plumbers, or secretaries. It leaves such decisions to the marketplace.[7]

Conclusion

I have offered several theoretical arguments that question the key assumptions upon which the case for comparable worth depends. These assumptions are either fallacious or they cannot be carried out in the real world without producing chaos. (1) Jobs have no intrinsic worth or value, and, therefore, they cannot be objectively measured nor compared. (2) Comparable worth operates on principles that are antithetical to the market. Thus, one must choose either the market or comparable worth. (3) Discrimination is irremediable, and it cannot be eliminated by comparable worth schemes. In fact, comparable worth might exacerbate the problem of discrimination by replacing the choices of millions of individuals by the view of "experts." (4) Finally, equality of opportunity is preferable on many grounds to the alternative embodied in comparable worth—equality of results.

Why the Market is Appealing

In the previous section, I argued that comparable worth and the market are incompatible, that they operate on different underlying principles, and that comparable worth is a slippery slope toward central planning and a command economy. Now, I would like to sketch several reasons why a market system ought to be appealing to those who both value liberty and human flourishing.

Markets are Just

In a market system, everyone is free to produce what he likes, to trade with other willing partners, and to give or bequeath his wealth to anyone he chooses. The system is based on a simple and just principle—that those who produce are entitled to the products of their labor. John Locke, the political philosopher who most influenced our Founding Fathers, understood well that by defending a right to property he was also defending the rights of life and liberty. Very often, he spoke only of property, meaning by it to include the other two rights. Where property rights are insecure, and even more where they are abrogated, liberty will not long survive. We have seen this truism borne out time and again; in fact, too many times for any reasonable person to doubt its veracity. From Russia to China, from Ethiopia to Cuba, from East Germany to Mozambique, deprivation of economic liberty has meant the death of liberty. Despite great differences in culture, state of development, geographical locale, and racial composition between these countries, the result has always been the same.

Another feature of the market system deserves more attention than it has received thus far in the debate over comparable worth. The ''market system'' is not really a ''system'' at all, in the sense that a system implies something designed or ordered—like a game, with rules handed down by a creator. Rather, the market—and this is one of Friedrich Hayek's great insights—is a ''spontaneous order.'' It results from not interfering with people and letting them do what they want, what they freely choose to do, in the absence of the initiation of force. Thus, capitalism, rightly understood, is just what people do when you leave them alone to do anything that is peaceful, or, in Lockean terms, anything that does not invade the like rights of others.

Comparable worth, however, would deprive individuals of an important component of this liberty of action by denying them part of their contractual liberty. This liberty, it should be noted, involves no force by one party upon another, and thus comparable worth would breach the spontaneous order by initiating the use of compulsion. To be more specific, comparable worth would deprive employers of the liberty to freely dispose of their property: to decide how much they are willing to spend on a particular type of labor.

One group of women who would be harmed if comparable worth artificially inflated entry-level salaries are women entrepreneurs, especially those in the process of creating new businesses, since these start-up companies are usually quite labor intensive. But even more significantly, comparable worth would deny many workers the liberty to negotiate contracts with potential employers. Just as minimum wage laws prevent unskilled teenagers—particularly those from minority groups—from gaining entry-level working experience by agreeing to work at low wages, comparable worth would price the labor of many women beyond their economic worth to employers. These women would be denied their basic economic liberty to freely negotiate contracts.

Comparable worth supporters would in all likelihood deride this argument: "What value is a liberty that lets women work at wage levels that are so low they are demeaning?" However, to women reentering the labor market after a marriage has broken up, to women just out of high school, to newly arrived immigrants, and to those with little skill, the freedom to take the clerical, factory, and sales jobs is the difference between having a chance to better themselves or being condemned to dependency. Comparable worth, by artificially raising the wages of such jobs, would restrict the number of such positions and make the lot of the poorest and least skilled women that much worse. This is neither just nor expedient.

Markets Express Consumer Sovereignty

Employers are consumers of labor, but they are also intermediaries between the ultimate consumers of their products and their laborers. Employers produce goods by combining various factors of production, and they hope these goods will mesh with what consumers want. They do so as efficiently as their competitors, or else they are soon out of business. Thus, comparable worth is not simply an attempt to replace the decisions of employers with the decisions of "experts," bureaucrats, and judges: Comparable worth seeks ultimately to replace the decisions of consumers themselves about how they wish to spend their money.

To most comparable worth advocates, those who embrace comparable worth because they see it as a means for bettering women's earnings, the tendency of comparable worth to undermine consumer sovereignty ought to be disturbing. Women are consumers, and they ought to value the liberty that has created the abundance we all enjoy. The more radical supporters of comparable worth, however, understand that the concept is a wedge they can use to undermine our free market economy, and I expect that they are not at all disconcerted by the tendency of comparable worth to replace the choice of consumers with the opinions of "experts." These radicals constitute, however, only a small proportion of those who support comparable worth.

Markets are Impersonal

If secretaries and nurses on average receive lower salaries than accountants and auto mechanics, it is not because any one group of "experts" has determined that the latter are more worthy than the former. It is simply a function of supply and demand. While individual employers may operate their businesses as idiosyncratically as they like (within, of course, the current labor and civil rights laws of the United States), they follow discriminatory wage policies at their peril. If fewer women choose to become nurses and secretaries, these occupations will receive higher remuneration in the future.

To condemn the marketplace because some employers discriminate, as comparable worth does, and to expect that a system that eliminates discrimination can be devised, is to search for the Holy Grail. Such utopian quests typically end in disaster, in inflicting on human beings infinitely worse suffering than they endured before the revolutionaries tried to remake mankind. Our collective experience as a species with attempts to better society by placing decisions in the hands of enlightened experts, those who know the truth, have all been colossal failures. The record of revolutionary societies in our century in the treatment of minorities is much worse than the record of free-market societies, South Africa included. If one doubts this, examine the lot of the Chinese in Vietnam, the Crimean Tatars, Jews, Germans, and other non-Russian peoples in the Soviet Union, the Turks in Bulgaria, the Hungarians in Rumania, the Eritreans in Ethiopia. . .

My purpose in adverting to this list of human atrocities is not to equate support for comparable worth with support for the Gulags. Rather, I would caution the supporters of comparable worth that the attempt to make society dramatically better by perfecting the results of the free choices of real people is more often than not—dare I say, always—calamitous. Those we place in power to perfect us are human, too, and whatever failings they have tend to be magnified by the possession of power over other people's lives. To the extent that comparable worth replaces impersonal market forces with the opinions of ''experts'' it flirts with the potential of doing great harm.

Markets are Efficient

In contrast to centrally planned economies, which have proven notoriously inefficient, market systems produce bounties undreamt of in past centuries. Comparable worth seems to require courts or wage boards to intervene continuously in the operations of all firms. With all the disruptions and inefficiencies such intervention would cause, a movement to explicit central planning of the economy would be the logical next step. Something would have to provide a ''cure'' for the dislocations caused by perpetual comparable worth evaluations, and since the market is out, central planning would be the only logical alternative.

Some supporters of comparable worth might respond: ''But even if comparable worth or central planning would be less efficient, if it achieves greater equality for women we would be willing to sacrifice efficiency to achieve this higher goal.'' Then the question would be, do centrally directed societies achieve greater equality for women in the work place?

A brief examination of the status of women in the Soviet Union would lead one to surmise that they do not. While it is difficult to get accurate statistics on the Soviet economy, Mervyn Matthews, Reader in Soviet Studies at the University of Surrey, has managed to piece together through émigré studies and official sources a picture of women's working life in that country.[8]

Equal pay provisions and a prohibition against discrimination between men and women performing the same work exist by law, but so do legal restrictions on women performing many dangerous or arduous jobs, working on night shifts, or lifting heavy burdens. A study of working women, émigrés from the Soviet Union living in Israel, showed that in their last year in Russia (1973), wives in full-time employment earned on average only 59% as much as their husbands. In his own émigré study, Matthews found a slightly lower wage gap, with women earning 71% as much as men. Women predominate in such occupations as trade and catering (83%), health and social security (82%), education (75%), and culture (74%). All of these categories of employment, Matthews notes, fall at the very bottom of the charts ranking occupations by earnings. Within any given sector, also, women are found to dominate the lowest skill categories. Women are congregated in such low-paid 'specialist' branches as medicine (68%). Women comprise 75% to 85% of service personnel and 60% of office staffs. The workload of women at home is twice as large as that of their husbands, with women spending over 25 hours each week on household tasks (excluding child care) and men about 11 hours. These figures would be considerably higher for the Soviet countryside, where household amenities such as running water are usually nonexistent.[9]

This picture looks remarkably familiar. What we would give up in the transition toward socialism would be a great deal of efficiency—much of women's time in the Soviet Union is taken up by standing in lines for the basic necessities of life—to say nothing of liberty. And the payoff seems trifling, if the Soviet example carries any weight.

Markets Allow Freedom of Exit and Entry

If a woman does not like the terms of employment offered to her, if she thinks the proffered wage is too low, she is perfectly free to seek another employer or strike out on her own. No one is perpetually tied to a job, as has been the practice off and on in some centrally planned economies. If one feels that as a secretary one is being discriminated against in relation to an office manager, one can acquire new skills and become an office manager or go into an entirely different line of work.

Comparable worth's advocates deride such a fluid vision of women's choices: "Aren't women stuck in the low-paying jobs they've trained for? Millions of women have invested their time in becoming nurses, secretaries, teachers, and social workers. Let's make sure they are paid more; let's not demand that they change their occupations."

Where this line of argument misfires is in assuming that millions of women would have to change jobs to increase their wages. This simply is not true. If enough women (at the margin, to use the economist's term) moved out of these jobs, or more realistically, if younger women did not replace their departing older sisters in sufficient numbers, the wages for those remaining would rise—without comparable worth and just as a result of natural market forces.

Women should not expect to eat their cake and have it too. If they want to flock to these traditionally female occupations—for some perfectly good reasons relating to family responsibilities—they should understand that one of the drawbacks to making the same choice as millions of others is that one contributes to the oversupply of labor in one's chosen field. Men know this. If there are too many middle managers and the economy takes a nose dive, then middle managers will be pounding the pavement. If there are too many lawyers, their salaries will decline.

As free individuals, women have choices. Older women, if they are dissatisfied with their salaries as teachers or nurses, can retrain for other more lucrative jobs or can start businesses of their own, as indeed, many of them have done. Younger women can train for traditionally male occupations, as indeed, millions of them have. To insist, as comparable worth activists do, that women are entitled to remain secretaries and nurses, but that their pay should be jury-rigged upward, is to appear childish, dependent, and unknowledgeable about how the world of work functions.

The Market and Women

Why should the market system appeal to women? The market has proven remarkably adaptable to the huge influx of women into the work place in the last few decades. In 1960, only 38% of women worked, while in 1983, 53% were employed. Many of these women formerly were homemakers with minimal or atrophied job skills.

Employment opportunities have multiplied to meet this rising demand by women for work outside the home. With relatively little dislocation, the market has expanded to provide jobs for women who now want to or need to work. Also, as aspirations of women have changed in the last fifteen years, largely as a result of the women's movement, women pioneers entered formerly male professions. Today, the pioneering phase is over, and it is no longer cause for celebration or even much notice when a woman is a lawyer, doctor, politician, business executive, coal miner, or truck driver.

The entry of women into the professions in great numbers and over such a short period of time has been truly astounding. The table below compares the percentages of women receiving master's degrees (or JD's in the case of law) in the professions in 1973 and 1983.

At the bachelor degree level, the representation of women receiving degrees is approaching parity in some professions: 45% in accounting, 42% in business and management, 41% in data processing, 49% in personnel management and pharmacy. Advertising and journalism degrees were awarded over 60% of the time to women.

These changes have been nothing short of revolutionary, except they have occurred without a revolution, imperceptibly, one woman's choice exercised at a time. We ought not to dwell upon the past, as comparable worth's supporters do to an excessive extent in their seeming obsession with past injustices and the putative discriminatory animus they incorporate into the marketplace. If women of another generation wanted to remain at home tending to their children, and their husband's salaries provided the surplus allowing them to do so, then it is foolish to blame "society" for the results. For society is nothing more than the attitudes and expectations of men and women who inhabit it at any particular time.

If men formerly saw women primarily as homemakers, so did women. Today, not only have the attitudes of women changed, but so has the perception of women by men. It does not require any elaborate empirical study to observe that younger men hold vastly different expectations of women than did their fathers and certainly their grandfathers.

Rather than bemoaning "societal values" of past generations or seeking an

TABLE 4.1
Women Training for the Professions[10]

	1973	1983
Accounting	8.7	34.4
Advertising	22.2	55.2
Banking and Finance	3.3	27.7
Business and Management	4.9	28.9
Computer and Information Sciences	10.6	28.3
Data Processing	4.9	20.6
Engineering	1.7	9.3
Journalism	35.1	53.9
Law	8.0	36.1
Personnel Management	7.1	39.3
Pharmacy	21.6	37.2

unattainable goal of eliminating all discrimination or trying to overturn our market system, women ought to encourage each other to become prepared for better and different jobs and to take more risks by becoming entrepreneurs.

Comparable worth is a detour—not to say, a dead end—that will not aid women in the long run, will not encourage them to pursue new paths, to explore new possibilities. Rather than condemning the market system, feminists ought to be glorying in it, for it has proved remarkably adaptable to women's evolving desire to work full-time, to work throughout their lives, and to work in new and challenging jobs. Why do comparable worth supporters view women as requiring special dispensations from government to advance in the marketplace, precisely at the time when women have made such great advances in the professions, in business, and in nontraditional vocations? Why emphasize women's disadvantages—their alleged victimization, their helplessness—when feminism rightly understood should glory in women's remarkable advances?

Indeed, it is the opponents of comparable worth, rather than its advocates, who have a positive attitude toward women's abilities, who see women as capable of determining what is in their own best interests and of competing and working for these goals in the marketplace alongside men, without any special privileges.

Notes

1. John Stuart Mill, *Principles of Political Economy*, Book I, chap. ii, par. 4; as quoted in F. A. Hayek, *The Road to Serfdom* (Chicago: University of Chicago Press, 1944), p. 112.
2. Hayek, *Road to Serfdom*, p. 122.
3. I do not intend to ignore the Wagner Act and minimum wage laws, which had already greatly circumscribed employers' latitude in compensating employees.
4. Robert Nozick, *Anarchy, State, and Utopia* (New York: Basic Books, 1974), Part II.
5. William R. Beer, "The Wages of Discrimination," *Public Opinion*, July/August 1987.
6. I much prefer the version of equality known as equality before the law or equality of rights, the conception of equality held by the classical liberals and our Founding Fathers. All individuals ought to be treated fairly by the courts, all ought to be subject to the same laws. Black or white, male or female, should make no difference before the law: justice is blind. But for now, I will not insist upon my preferred view of equality over equality of opportunity, for the latter, defective as it is, is preferable to equality of results. See David Kirp, Mark G. Yudof, and Marlene Strong Franks, *Gender Justice* (Chicago: University of Chicago Press, 1986), for a defense of the liberal version of equality of opportunity. They see the role of government as one of freeing up the processes by which individuals make choices for themselves, not as altering societal outcomes as these vary by sex.
7. This is a bit of an oversimplification. Part of the reason I would reject equality of opportunity as an ideal is that it tends to slide into equality of results, as I indi-

cated at the end of the last section. Attempts to correct the playing field do not have any natural cut-off point: do we stop when government forbids hiring discrimination; or do we go on to equalize incomes and confiscate inheritances so that all can start competing for jobs on an equal footing?

8. Mervyn Matthews, *Poverty in the Soviet Union: The Life-styles of the Underprivileged in Recent Years* (Cambridge: Cambridge University Press, 1986) pp. 37-39, 97-99.

9. For more on women in the Soviet work place, see: Gur Ofer and Aaron Vinokur, "Work and Family Roles of Soviet Women: Historical Trends and Cross Sectional Analysis," 3 *Journal of Labor Economics* S328 (1985). They found that Soviet women shared with women in most industrialized countries a dramatic rise in labor force participation, but suffered more from the "contradictions" between work and family roles as a result of the lack of amenities to alleviate their chores at home. Women's wages are low relative to men's.

10. U.S. Department of Education, 1986; as summarized in *The Wall Street Journal*, March 24, 1986, p. 15D.

Conclusion

Why has comparable worth—a theory based on misconceived assumptions and dependent on equally faulty techniques for its implementation—gained such widespread support? To answer a question with a question: Why did the labor theory of value retain its appeal in some quarters long after its inadequacies had been exposed by economists?

What the two theories share, I suspect, is that their adherents have invested a great deal of psychological capital in their truth. By abandoning their cherished theory, the adherents would have to admit that much of their case against the marketplace, against capitalism, had been grounded on an erroneous theory. In the case of the labor theory of value, the error lay in thinking that commodities ought to exchange for the amount of labor invested in producing them, with the inference that labor deserved to receive the entire product. For comparable worth, the error lies in assuming that jobs have objective value that can be measured and compared, with the inference that if the price of labor in the marketplace differs from this ideal calculation, then the market is contaminated by discrimination and biased against women.

Both theories are fallacious, as are the inferences drawn from them, yet the labor theory still commands loyal disciples—mostly among Western intellectuals and not their counterparts in the East. I am afraid comparable worth may endure, despite the palpable error of its assumptions, and the tendency it would have to hobble our economy, to place crippling burdens on our courts, and to ultimately drag our society down the road toward central planning. Some of those who fervently believe in the justice of the case for comparable worth are so driven by hatred of capitalism that their devotion to the cause seems beyond rational argument, much like the devotees of the labor theory. For the rest, those who see comparable worth as a cure for the wage gap but not as a crusade, I hope reason will prove persuasive, as it did for the economics profession as it abandoned the labor theory in droves at the end of the last century.

Perhaps what disturbs me the most about comparable worth as a strategy for improving women's lives is that it is essentially backward looking. It harps on perceived injustices of the past—some real, some exaggerated, and some simply misdirected—and pleads for redress. A far more progressive strategy is to

131

forget the past and concentrate on the future. The focus should be on the over three million women who own their own businesses, on the women who have scaled the corporate ladders in the last decade, on the women who have entered the professions in remarkable numbers, and on the women who have pioneered in formerly male blue-collar bastions. With the equal opportunity protections that we already have in place—the Equal Pay Act and Title VII—older women should be encouraged to acquire new skills and younger women to train for traditionally male jobs. If they encounter discrimination in route, then let them bring suit. The time has passed for women to plead with men for a fair chance in the marketplace; they have that chance, and they should be encouraged to continue taking advantage of it. The choice seems obvious: retrogress with comparable worth, or progress with the market.

Comparable Worth
Publications Bibliography

Aaron, Henry J. & Cameran M. Lougy, *The Comparable Worth Controversy* (1986).

Ahmuty, Alice L., "Summary of Pay Equity/Comparable Worth Activities by State Governments," Congressional Research Service, The Library of Congress, 85-615 E.

Aldrich, Mark and Robert Buchele, *The Economics of Comparable Worth* (1986).

Alpert, Richard B., "Comments on *County of Washington v. Gunther*," 28 *N.Y. L. Rev.* 149 (1983).

Barrett, Nancy S., "Obstacles to Economic Parity for Women," 72 *Am. Econ. Rev.* 160 (1982).

Becker, Gary S., *The Economics of Discrimination* (1971).

Bellace, Janice R., "Comparable Worth: Proving Sex-Based Wage Discrimination," 69 *Iowa L. Rev.* 655 (1984).

"A Foreign Perspective," *Comparable Worth: Issues and Alternatives*, ed. E. Livernash (1980).

Bellak, Alvin O. et al., "Job Evaluation: Its Role in the Comparable Worth Debate," 12 *Pub. Personnel Management J.* 418 (1983).

Beller, Andrea H., "The Impact of Equal Opportunity Policy on Sex Differentials in Earnings and Occupations," 72 *Am. Econ. Rev.* 171 (1982).

Bergmann, Barbara R. "The Conditions Under Which Wage Realignment Under the Rubric of 'Comparable Worth' Makes Economic Sense" (unpublished).

Blaxall, Martha and Barbara Reegan, *Women and the Workplace* (1976).

Block, W. E. and M. A. Walker, *Discrimination, Affirmative Action, and Equal Opportunity* (1982).

On Employment Equity (*Focus* No. 17 of The Fraser Institute). (1985).

Blumrosen, Ruth G., "Wage Discrimination, Job Segregation and Women Workers," 6 *Women's Rights L. Rep.* 19 (1980).

Boone, Carol, "The Washington State Comparable Worth Story," condensed from "The Washington State Comparable Worth Trial—A Victory for Working Women," *Comparable Worth Project Newsletter*, Spring, 1984.

Brennan, E. James, "Compensation $," 63 *Personnel J.* 56 (1984).

Brown, Judith Olans, et al., "Equal Pay for Jobs of Comparable Worth," 21 *Harvard L. Rev.* 127 (1986).

Bunzel, John H., "To each according to her worth?" 67 *Public Interest* 77 (1982).

Bureau of National Affairs, "Ninth Circuit Rejects Comparable Worth Theory," 53 *U.S. L. Week* 1013 (1984).

Pay Equity and Comparable Worth (1984).

"Sex Discrimination," 53 *U.S. L. Week* 2040 (1984).

Affirmative Action Today (with Appendix) (1986).

Burr, Richard E., "Are Comparable Worth Systems Truly Comparable?", Formal Publication No. 75 of the Center for the Study of American Business, July 1986.

"Rank Injustice," *Policy Rev.* 73 (Fall 1986).

"A Business Group Fights 'Comparable Worth'," *Business Week*, November 10, 1980, at 100.

California Commission on the Status of Women, "Pay Inequities for Women: Comparable Worth and Other Solutions," August 1983.

Carter, Michael F., "Comparable Worth: An Idea Whose Time Has Come?" 60 *Personnel J.* 792.

"Comparable Worth, Disparate Impact, and the Market Rate Salary Problem," 71 *Calif. L. Rev.* 730 (1983).

Cook, Alice H., "Comparable Worth: Recent Developments in Selected States," 34 *Labor L. J.* 494 (1983).

Cooper, Janet C., "Occupational Segregation and Wage Discrimination," 4 *Detroit C. L. Rev.* 1137 (1983).

Coval, S. C. and J. C. Smith, "Compensation for Discrimination," 16 *U.B.C. L. Rev.* 71 (1982).

Cowley, Geoffrey, "Comparable Worth: Another Terrible Idea," *The Washington Monthly*, January 1984, at 52.

Davidson, Marilyn J. and Cary L. Cooper, "Working Women in the European Community—The Future Prospect," 16 *Long Range Planning* 49 (1983).

DeForrest, Sean, "How Can Comparable Worth Be Achieved?" 62 *Personnel* 4 (1984).

Democratic Party, "Text of 1984 Democratic Party Platform," *CQ Almanac* 73-B (1984).

Dickman, Howard, "Exclusive Representation and American Industrial Democracy: An Historical Reappraisal," V *J. Lab. Research* 325 (1984).

England, Paul, et al., "Skill Demands and Earnings in Female and Male Occupations," 66 *Sociology and Social Research* 147 (1982).

"Equal Pay, Comparable Work, and Job Evaluation," 90 *Yale L. J.* 657 (1981).

Eyde, Lorraine D., "Evaluating Job Evaluation: Emerging Research Issues for Comparable Worth Analysis," 12 *Pub. Personnel Management J.* 425 (1983).

Fallows, Deborah, *A Mother's Work* (1985).

Fernandez, Julie A., "Letters to the Editor," 61 *Harv. Bus. Rev.* 194 (1983).

Ferraro, Geraldine A., "Bridging the Wage Gap," 39 *American Psychologist* 1166 (1984).

Fischer, Russell G., "Pay Equity and the San Jose Strike," 106 *Library J.* 2079 (1981).

Flick, Rachel, "The New Feminism and the World of Work," 71 *Public Interest* 33 (1983).

Freed, Mayer G. and Daniel D. Polsby, "Comparable Worth in the Equal Pay Act," 51 *U. Chi. L. Rev.* 1078 (1984).

Fulghum, Judy B., "The Newest Balancing Act: A Comparable Worth Study," 63 *Personnel J.* 32 (1984).

Gerson, Kathleen, *Hard Choices* (1985).

Gold, Michael Evan, *A Dialogue on Comparable Worth* (1983).

"A Tale of Two Amendments: The Reasons Congress Added Sex to Title VII and Their Implication for the Issue of Comparable Worth," 19 *Duq. L. Rev.* 453 (1981).

Golper, John B., "The Current Legal Status of 'Comparable Worth' in the Federal Courts," 34 *Labor L. J.* 563 (1983).

Greenwood, Daphne, "The Institutional Inadequacy of the Market in Determining Comparable Worth," XVIII *J. of Econ. Issues* 457 (1984).

Gregory, R. G. and R. C. Duncan, "Segmented Labor Market Theories and the Australian Experience of Equal Pay for Women," *J. of Post Keynesian Economics* 403 (1981).

"Women in the Australian Labor Force," 3 *J. of Labor Economics* 1 (1985).

Grune, Joy Ann and Nancy Reder, "Addendum—Pay Equity: An Innovative Public Policy Approach to Eliminating Sex-Based Wage Discrimination," 13 *Pub. Personnel Management J.* 70 (1984).

"Pay Equity: An Innovative Public Policy Approach to Eliminating Sex-Based Wage Discrimination," 12 *Pub. Personnel Management J.* 394 (1983).

Hacker, Andrew, "Women at Work," 33 *The New York Review of Books* 13 (August 14, 1986).

Hayek, F.A., *The Road to Selfdom* (1944).

Hewlett, Sylvia Ann, *A Lesser Life* (1986).

Hildebrand, George H., "The Market System," *Comparable Worth: Issues and Alternatives*, ed. E. Livernash (1980).

Hubbard, Givens & Revo-Cohen, Inc., "Pay Equity Trends" (Newsletter), September, 1984.

Hurd, Sandra, et al., "Comparable Worth: A Legal and Ethical Analysis," 22 *Am. Bus. L. J.* 417 (1984).

Illinois Commission on the Status of Women, "A Study of Job Classifications Currently Used by the State of Illinois to Determine if Sex Discrimination Exists in the Classification System," June, 1983.

Jacobsen, Aileen, *Women in Charge* (1985).

Jaussaud, Danielle P., "Can Job Evaluation Systems Help Determine the Comparable Worth of Male and Female Occupations?" XVIII *J. of Econ. Issues* 473 (1984).

Johansen, Elaine, "Managing the Revolution: The Case for Comparable Worth," 4 *Rev. of Pub. Personnel Ad.* 14 (1984).

J. K., "Discrimination," 6 *Am. J. of Trial Advocacy* 505 (1983).

Johnson, Craig E., "The Prima Facie Case of Comparable Worth," 11 *Ohio N. U. L. Rev.* 37 (1984).

Kalet, Joseph E., *Age Discrimination in Employment Law* (1986).

Kirp, David L., Mark G. Yudof, and Marlene Strong Franks, *Gender Justice* (1986).

Kondratus, Anna S. and Eleanor Smeal, "Comparable Worth: Pay Equity or Social Engineering?", Heritage Lecture 63 (1986).

Koziara, Karen S., et al., "The Comparable Worth Issue: Current Status and New Directions," 34 *Labor L. J.* 504 (1983).

Krauthammer, Charles, "From Bad to Comparable Worth," *Regulation*, July/August 1984, reprinted from *The New Republic* (1984).

Ladd, Helen F., "Equal Credit Opportunity: Women and Mortgage Credit," 72 *Am. Econ. Rev.* 166 (1982).

Landau, C. E., "Recent Legislation and Case Law in the EEC on Sex Equality in Employment," 123 *Int'l Labour Rev.* 53 (1984).

Levin, Michael, "Comparable Worth: The Feminist Road to Socialism," *Commentary*, September 1984, at 13. Also, in response to this article, "Letters from Readers," *Commentary*, January 1985, at 10.

Levine, Edward L., Book Review (*A Dialogue on Comparable Worth* by Michael Evan Gold), 37 *Personnel Psychology* 150 (1984).

Livernash, E. Robert (ed.), *Comparable Worth: Issues and Alternatives*, 2d ed. (1985).

Mahoney, Thomas A., "Where Do Compensation Specialists Stand on Comparable Worth?" 16 *Compensation Review* 27 (1984).

Mallison, Mary B., "Reason for Thanksgiving: Comparable Worth" (Editorial), *Am. J. of Nursing*, November 1981, at 2009.

Manhattan Institute, 4 *Manhattan Report on Economic Policy* 3 (1984), Interviews with June O'Neill, Robert Higgs, Joan Kennedy Taylor, and a Roundtable Discussion.

Mansbridge, Jane J., *Why We Lost the ERA* (1986).

McArthur, Leslie Zebrowitz, "Social Judgment Biases in Comparable Worth Analysis," *Comparable Worth: New Directions for Research*, ed. H. Hartmann (1985).

McBroom, Patricia A., *The Third Sex* (1986).

McCrudden, Christopher, "Equal Pay for Work of Equal Value: the Equal Pay Amendment Regulations," Pt. 1, 12 *Indus. L. J.* 197 (1983); Pt. 2, 12 *Indus. L. J.* 50 (1984).

Mutari, Ellen, et al., "Equal Pay for Work of Comparable Value," 73 *Special Lib.* 108 (1982).

National Commission on Working Women, "Women at Work," Winter 1986.

National Committee on Pay Equity, "The Wage Gap: Myths and Facts," (undated).

Ofer, Gur and Aaron Vinokur, "Work and Family Roles of Soviet Women: Historical Trends and Cross-Section Analysis," *J. of Labor Econ.*, January, 1985 at S328.

O'Neill, June, "An Argument for the Marketplace," *Society* 55 (July/August 1985).

"Earnings Differentials: Empirical Evidence and Causes," *Sex Discrimination and Equal Opportunity*, ed. R. Weitzel (1984).

"Role Differentiation and the Gender Gap in Wage Rates," *Women and Work*, ed. L. Larwood et al. (1985).

"The Trend in the Male-Female Wage Gap in the United States," 3 *J. of Labor Econ.* S91 (1985).

Pauley, Judith Ann, "The Exception Swallows the Rule: Market Conditions as a 'Factor other than Sex' in Title VII Disparate Impact Litigation," 86 *W. Va. L. Rev.* 165 (1983).

Pear, Robert, "Women Vow to Push Pay Equity Fight After Losing Court Ruling," *The New York Times*, September 6, 1985.

Pierson, David A., et al., "Equal Pay for Jobs of Comparable Worth," 12 *Pub. Personnel Management J.* 445 (1983).

Plender, Richard, "Equal Pay for Men and Women: Two Recent Decisions of the European Court," 30 *Am. J. of Comparative L.* 627 (1982).

Polachek, Solomon William, "Differences in Expected Post-School Investment as a Determinant of Market Wage Differentials," 16 *Internat'l Econ. Rev.* 451 (1975).

"Potential Biases in Measuring Male-Female Discrimination," 10 *J. Hum. Resources* 205 (1975).

Powers, Thompson N., "An Idea with a Long Way to Go," 70 *A. B. A. J.* 16 (1984).

Remick, Helen (ed.), *Comparable Worth & Wage Discrimination* (1984).

Ricardo-Campbell, Rita, "Women and Comparable Worth," Hoover Institution Monograph Series (1985).

Roback, Jennifer, *A Matter of Choice*, The Twentieth Century Fund, Inc. (1986).

Rosen, Benson, et al., "Compensation, Jobs, and Gender," *Harv. Bus. Rev.*, July/August 1983 at 170.

Rubin, Mary, Book Review (*A Dialogue on Comparable Worth* by Michael Evans Gold), 21 *Soc. Sci. J.* 22 (1984).

Rytina, Nancy F., "Earnings for Men and Women: a look at Specific Occupations," *Monthly Labor Rev.* 25 (1982).

Sampson, Charles, "The Role of the Personnel Manager in Comparable Worth, Job Evaluation, and Compensation Determinations," Center for Policy Studies and Program Evaluation, paper presented at the 1985 Midwest Political Science Association Meeting, April 17-20, 1985.

Sape, George P., "Coping with Comparable Worth," *Harvard Bus. Rev.* 145 (May/June 1985).

Schlafly, Phyllis, "Shall I Compare Thee to a Plumber's Pay,?" *Policy Rev.*, Winter 1985 at 76.

Schroedel, Jean Reith, *Alone in a Crowd* (1985).

Schwab, Donald P. and Dean W. Wichern, "Systematic Bias in Job Evaluation and Market Wages: Implications for the Comparable Worth Debate," 68 *J. of Applied Psych.* 60 (1983).

Schwab, Donald P. and Robert Grams, "Sex-Related Errors in Job Evaluation: A 'Real-World' Test," 70 *J. Applied Psychology* 533 (1985).

Seligman, Daniel, " 'Pay Equity' is a Bad Idea," *Fortune*, May 14, 1984 at 133.

Sigelman, Lee, et al., "The Salary Differential Between Male and Female Administrators: Equal Pay for Equal Work,?" 25 *Acad. of Management J.* 664 (1982).

Siniscalco, Gary R. and Cynthia L. Remmers, "Comparable Worth," 9 *Employee Rel. J.* 496 (1983).

"Comparable Worth in the Aftermath of *AFSCME v. State of Washington*," 10 *Employee Rel. J.* 6 (1984).

Sorensen, Elaine, "Equal Pay for Comparable Worth: A Policy for Eliminating the Undervaluation of Women's Work," 28 *J. of Econ. Issues* 465 (1984).

Steinberg, Ronnie, et al., *The New York State Comparable Worth Study Final Report* (1985).

Tenopyr, Mary L. and Paul D. Oeltjen, *Personnel Selection and Classification* (1982).

Thomas, Clarence, "Pay Equity and Comparable Worth," 34 *Labor L. J.* 3 (January, 1983).

Townshend-Smith, Richard, "The Equal Pay (Amendment) Regulations 1983," 47 *The Modern L. Rev.* 201 (1984).

Treiman, Donald J. and Heidi I. Hartmann (eds.), *Women, Work, and Wages* (1981).

Trost, Cathy, "More Family Issues Surface at Bargaining Tables as Women Show Increasing Interest in Unions," *The Wall Street Journal*, Dec. 2, 1986.

U.S. Commission on Civil Rights, *Comparable Worth: Issue for the 80's* (1984).

U.S. Commission on Post Office and Civil Service, "Equal Pay for Work of Comparable Value," Sept. 16-Dec. 2, 1982.

U.S. General Accounting Office, "Pay Equity," September 1986.

Vladek, Judith P., "Equal Access is Not Enough," 70 *A. B. A. J.* 16 (1984).

Volz, William H. and Joseph T. Breitenbeck, "Comparable Worth and the Union's Duty of Fair Representation," 10 *Employee Rel. J.* 30 (1984).

Waldauer, Charles, "The Non-Comparability of the 'Comparable Worth' Doctrine: An Inappropriate Standard for Determining Sex Discrimination in Pay," 3 *Population Research and Policy Rev.* 141 (1984).

Weiler, Paul, "The Wages of Sex," 99 *Harv. L. Rev.* 1728 (1986).

Weitzman, Lenore J., *The Divorce Revolution* (1985).

Wines, William A., "EEOC Conciliation Efforts in the Case Of the Willmar Eight," *Labor L. J.*, May, 1984 at 308.

Index